**"Okay, it looks like sponsorship, it feels like sponsorship...
but you're telling me..."**

T-Mobile Street Gig at the Natural History Museum, July 2006
One of ours!

Advertising and sponsorship have always been about using imagery to equate products with positive cultural or social experiences. What makes nineties-style branding different is that it increasingly seeks to take these associations out of the representational realm and make them a lived reality.

So the goal is not merely to have child actors drinking Coke in a TV commercial, but for students to brainstorm concepts for Coke's next ad campaign in English class… Disney transcends its sports network ESPN, a channel for guys who like to sit around in sports bars screaming at the TV, and launches a line of ESPN Sports Bars, complete with giant-screen TVs.

The branding process reaches beyond heavily marketed Swatch watches and launches 'Internet time', a new venture for the Swatch Group, which divides the day into one thousand 'Swatch beats'. The Swiss company is now attempting to convince the on-line world to abandon the traditional clock and switch to its time-zone-free, branded time.

From Naomi Klein's rejection of the branded world, 'No Logo',
still the best sponsorship primer in print …

Reproduced with the kind permission of Flamingo.

ten years of **red**mandarin

It's been ten years since Sally (Hancock) and Chris (Roe) set up Redmandarin and, although we're a self-effacing little business, we thought it was worth a celebration. Hence this book.

Sally meets Chris was essentially our original proposition: an excellent strategic understanding of sponsorship applied with the rigour of management consultancy to deliver impartial, world-class expertise.

Fundamentally, that hasn't changed. We're faithful to two founding beliefs: that sponsorship can be an enormously powerful marketing tool; and that most brands in sponsorship need a level of support beyond what's commonly available to really make their practice sing.

Redmandarin today is structured to offer our clients the benefits of a multi-disciplinary team focussing solely on 'sponsorship', with expertise in brand and management consultancy, research and evaluation, planning, media, events, channel marketing understanding – to ensure our sponsorship thinking maximises marketing ROI. Our approach to creative is similar: we work with a unique collection of partners to ensure our creative concepts are drawn from outside of the traditional box of tricks.

What has changed – and continues to change – is our vision, our thinking, our methodologies and our experience.

The other thing that's changed … is sponsorship.

why defining sponsorship?

Since 1999, sponsorship has evolved enormously. Then, if anything, there was wider concensus about the nature of sponsorship than now.

In 1999, and we're talking 25 years after the FIFA Argentina World Cup, which arguably first saw a structured, organised packages of 'rights' made available in a shape we would recognise today, sponsorship was still largely defined by the price of your rights.

We're talking only 15 years after the 1984 Atlanta Olympic Games and the formation of the IOC's sponsorship and broadcast offering, a period of intense rights inflation, driven by the TV landgrab inspired by BskyB's brilliant 1992 seizure of the Premiership broadcast rights. The sponsorship model was dominantly TV driven.

And David Beckham was still at Man U.

How things have changed.

We think it's high time for a new definition.

So we asked 40 people their opinion on what lies at the heart of sponsorship, on what really makes it special as a marketing activity. We tried to gather informed perspectives from every side, in the hope that, somewhere in the middle, there might be a meeting, that we could develop a construct which would provide a definition to take us forward. And we did.

But enough from us for now, have a read...

perspectives

frank craighill

Chairman and CEO of Altis marketing LLC

Frank is Chairman and CEO of Altis marketing LLC, consulting with Olympic bid cities and Olympic Sponsors.

Previously Frank was Chairman of Helios Partners, representing Sochi's successful bid for the 2014 Winter Olympics. Before that he was Worldwide President of Octagon, and co-founded Advantage International and developed The Olympic Program.

Frank began his career as a lawyer, also spending several years as a correspondent in Vietnam.

The most dramatic change over the time that I have been in the sports marketing industry has been the acceptance of sponsorship as an important strategic marketing communications tool. In the early days of the industry, sponsorship suffered from being seen as how the chief executive likes to spend his time. If he was a golf fan or a tennis fan then his company would sponsor a golf or tennis event. There wasn't much discussion about return on investment. Today the numbers have gotten so big that the industry has been forced to focus on return. There's an interesting shift going on currently based upon the extraordinary segmentation that is taking place in the marketplace and the dilution of interest in terrestrial television; brands are being forced to be more targeted, particularly when trying to reach a younger audience who rarely watch television these days - the one thing they do watch is sport.

Fortunately, there is a realization within the sponsorship community that through the integration of its sponsorship a company can reach many different segments of the market. As a result, sponsorship is becoming more important not less. In addition, the industry has gotten better at determining and measuring return on their investment. Too often media value is a crutch: when the marketing director has to stand in front of his Board and justify the value the company's received for its sponsorship outlay, he thinks he must have some numbers. I remember that Mercedes, in the early years of their sponsorship of the ATP Tour, got their agencies to physically count the minutes their logo appeared on the television screen and did an equivalence evaluation based on the cost of a 30 second spot, then discounted that number by 90% and still found that they got two or three times what they had paid in value.

When we first founded ProServ in the early 70's, the whole industry was in its infancy in terms of the dollars involved in professional sports. The two major agencies at the time were ProServ and IMG. At Proserv we were primarily focused on how we could help with the development of a circuit of professional tennis events. At the time, we were able to assist in the creation of a tennis broadcast package on public television to expose the professional game and its sponsors. In the early days of professional tennis the players often were offered guarantees since there was no prize money. For example, we might get an offer of $25,000 in the form of a guarantee for the players and we would persuade the tournament director to put the $25,000 in the prize money because we were trying to help build a circuit of prize money tournaments. Since our first four clients were Arthur Ashe, Stan Smith, Bobby Lutz and Charlie Pasarell, this was very appealing to the tournament directors.

media value is a crutch

kevin roberts

CEO Worldwide of Saatchi & Saatchi

Kevin Roberts is CEO Worldwide of Saatchi & Saatchi, the world's fourth largest communications group. He is the author of three Saatchi & Saatchi books on brands and marketing. He is also a member of the Publicis Groupe Management Board.

Previously Kevin held leadership positions globally with premier brands, including Gillette and Pepsi. He is a former director of the New Zealand Rugby Union and current Chairman of the USA Rugby Board of Directors.

The ROI that sponsorship has to bother itself with has changed. Return on Involvement is where the game is going to be played and sponsorship will get obliterated if it measures itself as it does now on awareness and eyeballs, because those are the wrong, wrong measures in today's age. We've moved from the Attention Economy into an Attraction Economy. Whereas eyeballs mattered, the question now is how do you attract consumers to feel loyalty beyond reason? How do you develop priceless value? Can sponsorships demonstrate priceless value? Can they demonstrate purpose, enrichment and involvement?

What does women's tennis bring to Sony Ericsson in terms of involvement and enrichment or happiness or purpose to the base proposition? That is the question that women's tennis has to answer. Sponsorship is talking about the wrong stuff and some of the stories are juvenile. It's trying to compete with traditional media with the old-fashioned metrics, and it's going to lose. Sponsorships are all about emotion, yet most of them are still sold rationally. If I were a sponsorship property now I'd be investing my money in new techniques that attempt to measure emotional connectivity and predict involvement.

The reason brands are interested in music and sport is because they're shortcuts to people's hearts. Every brand has to deliver the rational stuff - product, performance, quality, distribution, at a price that is competitive. If it doesn't, it's dead. But in this economy that is not enough. It has to demonstrate that it's authentic,

> **what does women's tennis bring to Sony Ericsson in terms of involvement and enrichment or happiness or purpose to the base proposition? That is the question that women's tennis has to answer**

true and genuine - and certainly not manipulative. Consumers will get supremely tired, very quickly, about anything that is not authentic and deeply rooted in the brand. David Ogilvy said it very smartly 25 years ago - the consumer is not a moron, she's your wife. Sports fans are not morons but sometimes they get treated like it. Most of the great sponsorships are grounded in the fans.

Much of what Coca-Cola does in sport is really admirable because they do it from the fans' point of view. Toyota is another company that really gets sport sponsorship if you see what they do with Munster rugby and the Heineken cup. Some of the other stuff just tries hard but there is no link - and fans and consumers just look at it and say there's something wrong: it's not authentic or credible.

Nothing in marketing that we did over the last three years is going to necessarily sustain over the next three years. We are entering an era where consumers have all the power, because they have masses of information. The rules of marketing are about to change from demand and control to connectivity and collaboration. The best brands will look to collaborate with like-minded partners, who get that they are a triumvirate of property, brand and consumer, all as equal partners. Most sponsors come at this from the wrong end of the spectrum, focused on brand equity or financial return, and the consumer is treated like something at the end of the line.

peter r. franklin

Group Director, Worldwide Sports & Event Management for The Coca-Cola Company

Peter Franklin is Group Director, Worldwide Sports and Event Management for The Coca-Cola Company, managing the Company's relationships with its major global sports partners, including the IOC, FIFA and UEFA.

Peter has been with Coca-Cola for 15 years, previously in the Corporate Legal Division with primary responsibility for International Business Affairs. Peter formerly practiced law at the international law firm of Skadden, Arps, Slate, Meagher & Flom.

When Coca-Cola looks at a sponsorship, there has to be a particular role for us to play. If you could just as easily substitute one of the other sponsors into our space, then we're not really doing a very good job. There has to be something that is unique for us, in helping to triangulate between our brands, the property, and the consumer's passions. Any activation – whether it is ours or another sponsor's – that feels generic, not personalized for the brand, is not successful from my point of view.

We have had very long associations with FIFA and the Olympics. Going back to the beginning, it has always been about connecting with people around the world where they live, work, and play. One of the things that we can bring to the table for our rights-holder partners is our knowledge of how people tick, all across the world. Often times we have more knowledge of consumer behaviour in these territories than the rights-holders do, and that is an enormously powerful thing to be able to bring to a sponsorship. Our business is about understanding people's behaviour in virtually every country in the world - that's what we do. That knowledge can help rights-holders with their specific objectives. For example, over a number of years we have been helping the IOC in their aim of reconnecting with youth.

when Coca-Cola looks at a sponsorship, there has to be a particular role for us to play... something ... unique for us, ... helping to triangulate between our brand, the property, and the consumer's passion...

Another benefit that we can bring to our relationships with rights-holders is our global reach. For example, we can talk to FIFA about the 2010 World Cup in South Africa in a very informed way because it's a very strong market for us, one of our 10 largest markets around the world. The scope and sophistication of our business in that country allows us to bring a lot of value to our relationship with FIFA. This value extends beyond consumer marketing to other important areas such as public affairs and communication. That type of business intelligence is very valuable: an enormous contact book around the world because we sell over 1.5 billion servings of our product every day.

3

steve cumming

Global Category Director, Sponsorship, PR and Events at Diageo

Steve Cumming is Global Category Director, Sponsorship, PR and Events at Diageo.

He started with Grand Met as a Graduate trainee and happened to be in the brewing business when it was broken up in 1990 and has been in drinks since. He went on to Scottish Courage and Carlsberg via a number of mergers and acquisitions, before joining Coke in 2002 and moving to Diageo in 2008.

Sponsorship. There isn't a single definition, but the unique nature of sponsorship is in its relationships and shared IP. Great sponsorship is realised through great experiential delivery. How people perceive sponsorship is not where sponsorship is or should exist in the way brands connect with consumers.

Sponsorship at the outset was very transactional but it's gaining more acceptance as a mainstream marketing discipline. It's unique because, as a platform, it drives a number of other strategic investments. The debate used to be: advertising or sponsorship, but it's become a much more integrated discussion, as it should be. Passion Point investment enables your brand and business to cut through in ways that other business and marketing levers can't.

Why sponsorship is not better understood in some businesses, I don't know, but it deserves to have a better reputation. Which is why I'm still as passionate as ever, and remain focussed on what's great about it, and what can be great about it in the future. When it works it's phenomenal and done properly it should be a great part of your mix.

The essence of sponsorship is 'win win'. I fundamentally believe in the value of partnership. You seek out partnerships that add value to both brand propositions. Partnership might sound a bit utopian but my view is that sponsorship is relational asset management, which has to be driven by a need for that relationship, otherwise you'd go and do it yourself. Even if a brand drives an idea itself it needs a set of partnerships and relationships to bring it alive.

Like any relationship you have to be committed to working on it. You have to move past the transactional to the brand placing itself at the heart of a space and bringing media to the space as appropriate, as Orange have done with film. I really do admire Red Bull's approach and their sustainable commitment. There's an asset strategy that's really grown a brand.

My title at Coke was Head of Marketing Assets and Brand Experience. Coke get it. It is about leveraging your asset partnerships, to allow you to create the sort of experiential campaigns that deepen relationships. I don't see any significant differences with experiential. Marketing asset management doesn't take it far enough though, because it's a mindset you have to get into. I'd love not to use the word sponsorship, but you can't get away from it. You can't go into the marketplace and say I'm in Consumer Relational Asset Marketing, or not yet at least.

There's no way we want people just to drink a pint of Guinness, we want the brand – and the sponsorship experience - to be the enabler to a deeper emotional connection.

My task here at Diageo is to continue to change the mindset, to go from sponsorship to relational asset management, then build the sort of relationships which will drive value.

> **we want the brand - and the sponsorship experience - to be the enabler to a deeper emotional connection**

keld strudahl

Global Marketing Director at Carlsberg

Keld is Global Marketing Director at Carlsberg where he develops new commercial functions within marketing to support Carlsberg's Global Marketing Strategy. Keld joined Carlsberg 16 years ago working with international brands and marketing.

He has worked on some of the most prestigious Sports and Entertainment projects in the world including World Cups in football, basketball, athletics and skiing. Before joining Carlsberg, Keld Strudahl worked as a consultant in the advertising industry.

My background is MBA, CBS Copenhagen and a BA in the USA, various ad agencies, and Nielsen. Then Carlsberg offered me a position as either brand manager or with responsibility for sponsorship. I thought sponsorship could be a good opportunity - although I was doubtful. So that's how I ended up in this profession.

So I've been at Carlsberg since 1990 and had responsibility for many aspects of marketing, but sponsorship has always been my baby. The CEO when I joined really wanted to professionalise our approach. It was a challenge initially to answer where sponsorship fits into the overall mix, but we won acceptance eventually because we were able to measure its impact and to prove that sponsorship sold product. We've also been very critical of ourselves. We've done a lot of weeding out over the years, to find out that football and music work better than anything else for Carlsberg. And now we have people wanting to join us because of our sponsorships.

I'm particularly proud of our 2000 Euro campaign when we launched Part of the Game, as well as the approach we took to skiing. Not just about a banner on a hillside or endorsing an athlete but, taking our tagline, creating probably the best après ski in the world.

Nowadays, we're less involved with big creative campaigns. Creative campaigns get mixed results. More and more we make sure we really express ourselves as 'proud sponsor'. We don't need unique creative campaigns: we just need

to make sure we benefit from the contracts, so we're driven by sales promotion activities.

But we need to get away from the nasty word of sponsorship, to come up with a different word. I don't think that the word 'sponsorship' covers what we do today. Yes, we buy the rights to leverage a property but we also do so much more. Sponsorship is about partnership and about creating with our help an experience for the stakeholders i.e. consumers, customers.

I fear there are only so many 'interesting' sponsorships left. The big ones get bigger and the small ones get smaller - it's very polarising. What I'd like to see is smaller properties getting more professional and developing the confidence they can make a difference. And for sponsors to be willing to take smaller properties and develop them rather than hang on to the big ones. I certainly admire Red Bull for that: they've shown you can take a lot of smaller sponsorships, often quite strange activities, and make them work.

when you give the agencies the freedom to create a campaign similar in scope to our sponsorship, they find it very challenging

I've got a burning passion that sponsorship can make a difference in today's world of fragmented media. Do sponsorship right, find the right audience and sponsorship can make a big difference compared to traditional marketing. You're better off than running an advertising campaign which people forget after two months. And when you give the agencies the freedom to create a campaign similar in scope to our sponsorship, they find it very challenging.

tony ponturo

Founder and CEO of Ponturo Management Group, LLC

Tony Ponturo is the founder and CEO of Ponturo Management Group, LLC; a consulting, management and investment company in media, sports and entertainment.

Previously he was President and CEO of Busch Media Group and the Vice President of global media, sports and entertainment marketing of Anheuser-Busch Inc. overseeing broadcast exclusives in the Super Bowl, FIFA World Cup, USOC and Olympics and negotiating the first Dale Earnhardt Jr NASCAR team deal, Formula One and English Premier League sponsorships.

Over the last few years we started to pick up something from our sponsorship research that said the consumer more than ever questions the whole concept of Official Partnership. There was a time when they felt that because a brand was the official mobile phone or the official beer of the league, that it said something special about you. But now they realise that this was something that was purchased. It doesn't mean you are the best and that the league or team values you, but that you were just the guy who ponied up the money. This is troubling for rights-holders.

I think that the way in which sponsorship has been sold historically has damaged its reputation as a marketing tool.

> **there was a time when consumers.. felt that, because a brand was the official beer, it said something special about you - now they realise you were just the guy who ponied up the money**

The last five years has seen the demand for sponsorship and its price rise dramatically. It's been a very competitive environment: telecommunications companies grabbed sponsorship as a brand building tool, the automotive sector kept on spending a great deal of money, there was beer competition and soft drink competition. Money was plentiful all down the line. Sports properties particularly at the top end didn't have to put a great deal of effort into selling the sponsorships. They kept raising the price and getting the money. That led to a laziness being built into the culture, and that has weakened the product. It also means the come down is even harder as the market dries up.

The other implication of this selling mentality is that the leagues and clubs came across as greedy. The only message they were sending was, 'I need money to pay the high cost of business', which was primarily driven by athletes' salaries. They were saying that in order to keep moving forward they need more and more money. But their image is now out of tune with the times. Now the whole community of sport is getting a lesson in real economics, which is to say they have to sustain themselves on a more realistic basis. The days when they get by on the passion of sports are over and the whole sector is more accountable. If they come to sponsors and say they want a 20-25% increase, because their costs are going up, it will fall on deaf ears. Sponsors can't raise their product prices like that, the consumer won't accept it.

There has been little work done by the property side to help brands use sport to form the basis of a marketing strategy, other than saying, 'We want $30 million for the front of the shirt because... well, just because'. That doesn't work anymore.

patrick nally

Principal of EMC2 Ltd.

Patrick Nally has been widely credited as the 'Founding Father' of sports marketing since he established West Nally in the early 1970s. Patrick was involved in the creation of the General Association of International Sports Federations, and has worked closely with the International Olympic Committee since the 1970s.

Today, Patrick is a specialist consultant and lectures on sponsorship as a Touring Fellow of the World Academy of Sport. As the principal of ECM2 Ltd, Patrick is working with UNESCO on programmes to attract private sector support.

The fundamentals of sports marketing were laid down in the mid-1970s, and the same issue applies now as it did then, price still has nothing to do with a quantifiable return.

Coca-Cola's partnership with FIFA is where it all began. Until then Coke's involvement with sport, like that of every other sponsor, had been at a local level as there was no central marketing budget. When I went to Atlanta to offer Coke the opportunity of a global package, this was new territory.

This relationship created the global industry we know today. It meant that international federations such as FIFA and the IOC were able to sell themselves as truly global platforms. Coke was able to activate its marketing objectives globally using football to reach the world's youth. The impact of this shift in approach was hugely significant to the sports business we know today as the ceiling on rights values that had been in place was lifted.

The concept of the rights package grew from this moment. Stadium advertising had been controlled by television, the stadium owner or anybody who felt like sticking something to a wall. No thought had been given to what was sold in the stadium, as for the pouring of soft drinks, who cared? The Coca-Cola Company did. They also cared that every one of their global markets (all now paying for the rights to the FIFA relationship) wanted to promote their association with FIFA during the World Cup and expected it to be exclusive – no Pepsi – in any market. Every major rights-holder from the IOC to the IAAF adopted this model, but like all new developments it has a life cycle. My view is that the package concept is dying; and outside of

FIFA, UEFA and possibly the IOC, things are changing rapidly. Sponsors no longer want a packaged solution. They want bespoke, they want brand connection. They want sophistication, they want measurement, they want social responsibility, they want to be concerned about sustainability, education, heritage, living their ideals and being focused on corporate expenditure. This is sport's version of the 'circle of life', the sponsors want what we started with in the beginning, and they want sport to be 'a means of communication', to achieve their own bespoke goals and objectives, not just an off the shelf package.

The industry that has grown so fast over the past two decades is about to face its first big mid-life crisis. How it responds is the story of the next twenty years.

the package concept is dying

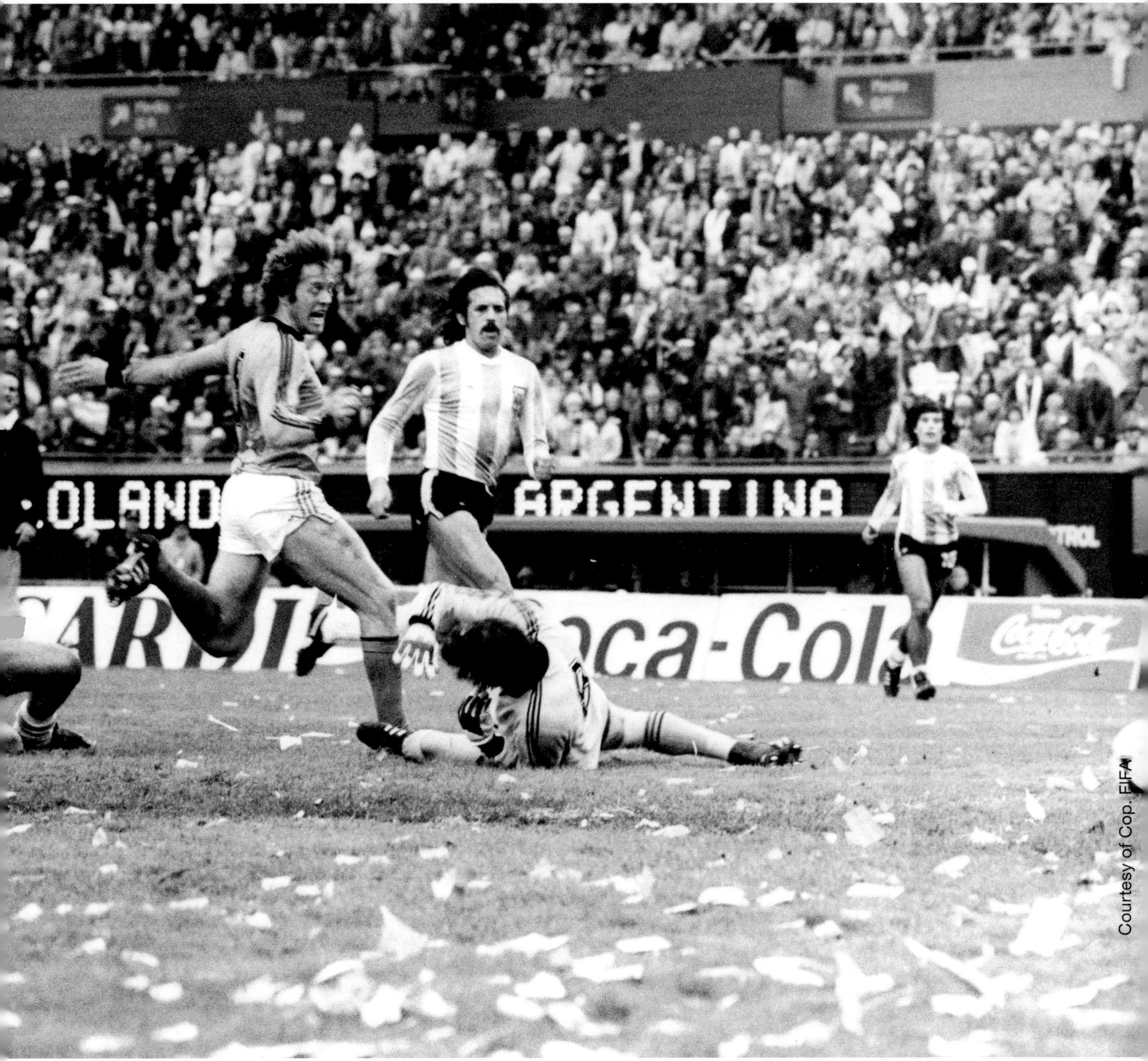

Courtesy of Cop. FIFA

john luff

Founder of Sustainable Marketing

John is the founder of Sustainable Marketing, helping organisations promote their brand, corporate social responsibility (CSR) and sustainability credentials. Previously John was Head of Global CSR and Head of Global Brand for BT, leading BT's sponsorship of the Global challenge. John has also held senior roles in occupational psychology and organisational development. He is an alumnus of the Prince of Wales Business and the Environment programme and a Founding member of the Superbrands CSR Advisory Panel.

There is a real trend all away from the 'how big is your willy?' sports sponsorships, the kind of nonsensical sponsorship that will always justify coming under the spotlight because it's not sustainable, not just from a green point of view, but because it never made any sense. Former wonder example, absolutely barking mad - Honda. Don't try and retrofit your objectives. If you want Formula One, do it, but don't try and claim you are doing it because you want to be green, it's barmy.

Sponsorship is better placed than any other marketing activity to link everything together. Why did you choose one particular charity or sponsorship over another? Why choose Spaces for Sport over leukaemia or AIDS research? The answer is usually because it was the whim of a previous director. Or, if you just give money to respond to the perception of consumers, it's guilt money. That doesn't work anymore: it has to be driven by your core business, so it's transparent.

The first thing a client often does is show me a list of good causes they want to support. That isn't a strategy, that's a shopping list. The question has to be: why are you doing this?

rights-holders are... competing with... people who can offer community-based engagement

Brands can't get away with just slapping their logo on a couple of favourite activities, whether it's charity or the arts. If people can look at what you are doing and understand why you're doing it, they will support it. Your employees need to be really engaged, and if I'm a customer can I get involved with it. The BT global challenge was a good example of this. 99% of the people who were involved weren't sailors. There is absolutely nothing wrong at all with good solid serious marketing being used to raise the profile of your brand. If you're doing it, why not talk about it?

There is a great deal of vested interest in the status quo, things have gone well over the last 10 years, money has flown in. If you are a sponsorship manager or a director of sport in a governing body, that is the world which you inhabit, that is the contact base you have, that's the website you read, you won't know any thing about other forms of sponsorship.

Many sports rights-holders are refusing to see what's happening; they're in a state of denial, as though, if they keep shouting long enough, it will somehow come right. And they will be blind-sided by the competition because the people they are now competing with are those that can offer community-based engagement, not charity but opportunities for employee volunteer systems. That is just more appealing than a chief executive writing a cheque.

Formula One is not that cutting any more.

The world's toughest yacht race

www.btchallenge.com

36

philippe le floc'h

Marketing Director at UEFA

Philippe is Marketing Director at UEFA, overseeing TV and media content strategies and their implementation as well as providing brand management and business research in-house services. Philippe joined UEFA as Senior Manager Marketing & TV and in 2004 became Director of the Marketing Division, directly reporting to the UEFA General Secretary. Previously, Philippe worked at ISL Marketing AG, a sports marketing agency whose partners included FIFA and UEFA; and at IMS, whose clients included the IOC.

When executed correctly, sport sponsorship creates a win-win situation for the sponsor as well as the rights-holder. But this goes far beyond the simple financial transaction in which the rights-holder receives a certain amount of money and the sponsor receives a set of rights, which if all goes to plan, allows him to increase his sales. It should be a win-win situation at a higher level too, for the sport itself. It is important that the coming together of business and governing body should enhance the sport, helping it to develop and grow. The expertise of the sponsor can play a key role in enhancing the profile of the sport and by so doing, the sponsor will be associated with a better property, one which enjoys a higher profile.

A good example of this type of partnership approach can be seen in Heineken's relationship with the UEFA Champions League. More specifically, witness the collaboration between the governing body UEFA and sponsor Heineken in organising and delivering the UEFA Champions League trophy tour.

Together with Heineken, the governing body takes the UEFA Champions League trophy to different parts of the world (outside Europe). In 2007 this was Asia, in 2008 South America and in 2009 the trophy travels to Africa.

By doing so, UEFA and Heineken bring the UEFA Champions League to those areas of the world which are usually deprived of the best club football in the world. It's amazing to see how popular football and the UEFA Champions League is in these countries. Long lines of kids, each dressed in their favorite team jersey, waiting sometimes for hours to have a picture taken with the trophy and feel a bit closer to the best club football in the world.

This is not a Heineken trophy tour but the tour is presented by Heineken. In that way Heineken has understood that they are the facilitators of the initiative, they are bringing the UEFA Champions League to the fans, rather than attempting to be perceived as the owners of the competition, trophy or tour. In this way, the trophy tour is not seen as a commercial initiative and so Heineken links in a more credible way to the values of the trophy and of the UEFA Champions League.

sport sponsorship … should be a win-win situation at a higher level too, for the sport itself

UEFA Champions League Trophy Tour
presented by ☆ Heineken

CHAMPIONS LEAGUE

paul meulendijk

Vice President, Head of Sponsorship for MasterCard Europe

Paul Meulendijk is Vice President, Head of Sponsorship for MasterCard Europe, overseeing the UEFA sponsorships for Champions League and Euro 2008 and MasterCard's European golf sponsorships.

Previously Paul was General Manager for Vicrea Solutions in the Netherlands and before that Group Director, Brand Management and Event Marketing for Nortel Networks. Over 13 years he has held various Marketing and Sales positions in the Netherlands, France, Switzerland, and the USA.

Sponsorships work best when they are integrated with all the other marketing disciplines at a brand's disposal. To do this effectively, there needs to be a strong overarching theme that allows the sponsorship to link through to areas such as advertising and direct marketing, and becomes a consistent line throughout everything you do. If, on the other hand, sponsorships take place in a separate environment, it becomes a competition between the various marketing disciplines within the company.

MasterCard's sponsorships utilise the 'Priceless' campaign as an overarching theme, allowing us to be more consistent and efficient in our communications across all our properties: from the UEFA Champions League and Euro Championships through to our golf, NBA and NFL properties. Across each of these sponsorships we are constantly looking at the return on objectives whilst simultaneously seeking to bring priceless experiences to customers.

During the UEFA EURO 2008, Austria and Switzerland offered, as one of the prizes through MasterCard and supporting banks, the red and yellow cards used by the match referees. We secured these via UEFA and the prizewinners met the referee of that evening's match, who handed over the cards they had used with their signatures on them. In one instance, the referee even took off his own shirt and signed it for the winner. The recipient was flabbergasted. This is what priceless is all about: things that money can't buy.

Through our sponsorships and by working with properties like The Champions League, we can create these kinds of moments and engage with our customers in a meaningful way; bringing something special that allows them to benefit from our involvement as an organisation.

During the UEFA EURO 2008 finals weekend, we were able to offer another priceless experience to a number of prizewinners from around the world: they were invited to meet our brand ambassador - the former Italian referee Pierluigi Collina - who was kind enough not only to meet and greet our prizewinners, but also to bring Roberto Rosetti, the referee for the final, to the meeting and introduce him to the winners.

Sponsorship, used this way, is not just a vehicle to promote the brand, but an opportunity to share moments with consumers and to link very closely to our business to become an integrated part of our marketing activity.

> **there needs to be a strong overarching theme that allows the sponsorship to become a consistent line throughout everything you do**

richard w. pound

O.C., O.Q., Q.C., FCA. Partner at Stikeman Elliott law-firm

Richard is partner at Stikeman Elliott law-firm and has been in Time Magazine's 100 most influential people in the world for his relentless efforts to rid sport of performance- enhancing drugs.

Richard was founding Chairman of the World Anti-Doping Agency. In 2008, he received the Laureus 'Spirit of Sport' Prize for his work as head of WADA. He is a member of the IOC and a director of the Vancouver Organising Committee for 2010.

Visa's partnership with the International Olympic Committee was hugely successful and an example of a transformational sponsorship. It started in the mid-1980s and at the time, the idea that they would sponsor sport was sort of counter-intuitive, because Visa has such a complex business model. We first tried to sell the credit card category to American Express, and they just laughed at us, turned us down flat, because of the price, and I guess they thought we would come crawling back.

The same thing happened with IBM. They said their business was mainframe computers, 'We're a business to business organisation', which is interesting given how the computer industry has developed.

By contrast, Visa worked out how they could align their deep, deep consumer reach - everybody has a Visa card - with the rights that they bought. They were also one of the first companies to become a TOP partner, itself a landmark moment in the development of the sponsorship industry.

The Los Angeles Olympics in 1984 was financed on the old model, but sowed the seeds for the development of the TOP programme. In '84, the Los Angeles Organising Committee fell out with the USOC when they signed up Fuji, which conflicted with Kodak's deal with the IOC sponsor. Kodak had sponsored the Olympics for many years and were in fact a sponsor of the 1896 Games, the first Games of the modern era. But Kodak wouldn't step up to the plate financially in LA.

> **Visa's partnership with the International Olympic Committee was hugely transformational**

When the dust settled, sponsors began telling us how hard it was to do business with the IOC and the Olympic movement, because of the way it was organised. Back then, before we developed the TOP programme, a sponsor with the local Games organising committee would have to go to every Olympic Committee in the world and make a separate deal for the rights to use the rings in their territory. This was too expensive and time-consuming and just not worth it. This was the light bulb moment and now the IOC's economic model is far healthier.

Think back to the 1980 Moscow boycott, when 95% of our income was coming from one source: television. And in turn 95% of that revenue was from one country: the United States. We realised that we had all our eggs in one basket, and were dominated by the country that tried to wreck the games in 1980. We had to find other sources of income and get a better geographic balance. Global companies began to see the benefits they could accrue by being associated with the Olympics.

simon lowden

Chief Marketing Officer for Pepsi International

Simon is Chief Marketing Officer for Pepsi International, developing, managing and executing beverage marketing strategies and programmes around the world. Previously he led the International Marketing team on CSD brands Pepsi, 7UP and Mirinda.

Simon first joined PepsiCo in 1996 as UK Marketing Director before moving into a European assignment, and then joining the international team in New York. He started his career at Unilever.

Pepsi's overriding philosophy is to partner with 'People who' rather than 'Institutions that'. When applied to football it means we want to be involved with players who do the stuff on the field, not with FIFA or UEFA - the governing bodies can feel very cold somehow.

The key to success lies in the activation, and by involving ourselves with players, we can activate into different parts of the world. It is this human element which makes us feel warm and cuddly towards a brand, rather than 'Oh no, here comes another corporate sponsorship'. The same applies to music. We preferred to create the Pepsi Chart Show rather than sponsor an existing show because it gave us the ability to work with great people and for them to grow with us.

Our relationship with David Beckham ran from 1997 to 2005, a time period over which he matured as a person and as a player, and was a great ambassador for us. We took him to China and Thailand and got him involved in our grassroots projects, so we gave kids from all over China access to David Beckham and at the same time we made him famous there.

When it works well, something like that becomes a very symbiotic relationship. It also means we can have English players and Brazilian players and Italian players, which makes it a very flexible platform. Whether it's Fabregas, Henry or Beckham we will commit to making them famous around the world, and making sure their shirt is sold for Arsenal or whoever, in Bangkok and Beijing. That partnership model is the way forward, not just 'we need two days of your time for an advertising shoot'.

Sponsorship properties have to think how they can be a partner that contributes to the greater good and unless you can demonstrably grow both businesses why would anyone get involved with you. FIFA and the IOC will struggle to continue to bring in multi-million dollar sponsorships unless they are prepared to be more of a partner with their sponsors.

What institutions like FIFA deliver is a halo effect - overarching critical mass. But what do you really get? You can get blocked seats for a game and you get the FIFA logo on pack, and that's about it. Then you can obviously pay to advertise in the stadium and around the town. In Beijing for the Olympics, Pepsi could not be seen in line of sight around the stadium, which is quite a powerful protection for Coke.

what institutions like FIFA deliver is a halo effect - but what do you really get?

But the research comes back that consumers think Pepsi is as much a sponsor of the World Cup as Coke. This is because the downside of a partnership with a body like FIFA, UEFA or the IOC is you get very little visibility. So unless you buy into the broadcast sponsorship, which is another load of cash, nobody knows you're there.

simon pestridge

Marketing Director for Nike UK & Ireland

Simon is Marketing Director for Nike UK and Ireland. He has worked at Nike in marketing roles for 14 years - in Consumer Research, Public Relations and Internal Communications, before starting in Brand Management in 2001, where he led the Football and Sport Culture brand strategies for Nike USA, then moving to Australia as Marketing Director for Australia/NZ and finally to his current role, most recently overseeing the launch of Nike PhotoiD, the mobile campaign promoting its footwear.

Sponsorship is not necessarily a word I would associate with what we do.

Nike provides answers to problems facing athletes. The fact that we do this on a global scale, with iconic individuals and teams, does not make it sponsorship. On any level you look at it, we are innovating to improve athletic performance. We use our relationships with athletes all over the world to eventually give any and every sportsperson competitive advantage.

Take someone like Cristiano Ronaldo, although there is obviously a contractual agreement between Nike and the player, the relationship is built on Nike's ability to help him to be better at what he does. If Cristiano wants a boot that will help him get in front of a defender and be quicker to the ball then we look to develop innovations that will solve that problem.

At the same time, the learnings from his input and feedback around product development helps us finally develop an innovative and in many cases lightweight piece of sport's design that is available to the consumer. The loop closes when consumers can reap the benefit, knowing that world-class sportspeople have helped inform the product that is available to them.

> **I'd argue that sponsoring events only allows you to have a coherent narrative with consumers around that event**

One of the sponsorships that's touched me personally - it sounds biased - but it's actually Nike's sponsorship of Lance Armstrong. As a lot of companies were bailing from him when he was diagnosed, our folks stood by him. That's what a relationship is all about and I struggle to think of anything else that comes close. But in terms of campaigns, I'm proudest of Nike's Scorpion Knockout in 2002, for the scale of what we achieved with an attitude that had never been seen before.

I'd argue that sponsoring events only allows you to have a coherent narrative with consumers around that event. Being entrenched within the sport, which very, very few brands have the ability or right to achieve, is the only way that you can have consistent dialogue with your consumers. Fortunately, Nike is a sports company and that gives us a legitimate voice within sport 24/7.

ade adepitan mbe

Paralympian basketball player

Ade was introduced to wheelchair basketball at the Stoke Mandeville Junior Games, and has now represented Great Britain at the Olympics in Athens and Sydney as well as winning at the World Championships.

In 2005, Ade was awarded an MBE for his contribution to disabled sport. He is well known as a motivational speaker and an Ambassador for the NSPCC as well as a Patron for The Association of Wheelchair Children and Scope.

To me, sponsorship was always personal. I used to sit with my mates and talk about wheelchair basketball and we would say, 'Wouldn't it be great if we could afford to make a career out of this'. Even then we knew that the only way that was going to ever happen would be because of sponsorship.

And the single most significant relationship to me and my friends was Michael Jordan and Nike. Growing up in the 1980s, adidas was the label to have, and back then they were outselling Nike two to one all over the world. The reason I wore Nike was because of him. I saved my money for months and months to get a pair of Air Jordans. They cost £100, a ridiculous price.

It wasn't just the Nike tick we were buying, but the logo of him flying through the air doing his 360 degree dunk. To me that logo is as famous as the McDonald's golden arches. We recognized it instantly. We bought his hats, the vest, the balls, everything. Most people only knew Michael Jordan because of Nike, they saw him in the adverts before they ever watched him play basketball. I can't think of any other athlete who was so synonymous with a brand. The guy has been retired over 10 years now and the two names are still tied together.

For us, in London, Nike was a very aspirational brand. By buying the trainers we were making a link to America and to the NBA and on to the streets; we were saying that we wanted to do a 360 degree dunk shot, just like him. His image reached out to different groups of people. I remember we'd see white middle-aged dudes wearing their white Nike Air Jordans with their suits, and look at each other as if to say, 'how crazy is that?'. That was the genius of it, they hit everybody, everyone bought into the idea.

It also had a profound effect on the image of basketball. There had been stars before, like Magic Johnson and Larry Bird, but Michael Jordan took it worldwide. Now when you go around the world you can see a Manchester United shirt or a David Beckham reference, whether you're in China or Africa. Ten years ago you could go to the same places and you would see people in the number 23. I've been to South America and South Africa and people are wearing Michael Jordan's shirt. He is the blueprint for every personal endorsement sponsorship that has followed.

the reason I wore Nike was because of him

david wheldon

Global Director of Brand, Vodafone Group

David is Global Director of Brand, Vodafone Group. Prior to joining Vodafone, he held senior positions on both sides of the marketing fence. Starting at Saatchi & Saatchi, he was then appointed Managing Director of Lowe Howard-Spink in London. He later became Global Director and VP of Advertising for the Coca-Cola Company under the aegis of Sergio Zyman. David then returned to the agency world as President of BBDO Europe and finally arrived at Vodafone via WPP.

I've been Global Brand Director for Vodafone for five years, but I started as an adman in the 80's at Saatchi and Saatchi, and then ran an agency at Lowe Howard Spink in the late 80's and early 90's. From 1993 to 1997, I was the Worldwide Director of Advertising for the Coca-Cola Company where of course we did lots of advertising for sponsorship properties. I certainly spent all of the 80's thinking sponsorship was a waste of money, a Chairman's indulgence and not capable of driving brand engagement, brand equity or all of those things I now know sponsorship to do very powerfully.

For a business like Vodafone which has partly grown through acquisition globally, there's nothing better for building name awareness. Across borders it's more efficient at awareness generation than advertising. Take Ghana for example, a new market for us – awareness of Vodafone as a brand already stood at over 50% before we even entered the market, and this can only come from our sponsorship.

I'm a total convert to sponsorship as a marketing platform and to drive engagement with the brand. A lot of marketing agencies still underestimate the power of sponsorship which is unwise of them. What sponsorship gives you is a very very rich ability to touch your customers. Coca-Cola's sponsorship strategy goes back to Woodruff, the original President. One of his famous lines was: 'we need to be within our arms' reach of desire', which drove both the distribution strategy and the sponsorship strategy. If you drill into Coke data, an awful lot of emotional engagement with the brand has come from sponsorship.

> **I'm a total convert to sponsorship as a marketing platform and to drive engagement with the brand**

These are tough times for rights-holders. Their expectations for rights fees are pretty steep. But against a recessionary backdrop, sponsorship needs to work very hard to show marketing return on investment and some of the metrics aren't quite what they could be. For the industry to thrive it needs to sharpen up its act. Measurement in particular is important for me. I know for example with every bone of my body that Lewis Hamilton wearing a Vodafone cap and suit branding creates a strong emotional connection with Vodafone but it's very difficult to show through the metrics. We can show the ROI, we can show the Preference Created but showing the emotional engagement is tougher.

Sponsorship's difficult to define. In short we look for the things that our customers are passionate about to indicate where we should think about being involved. For instance, this leads us to be heavily involved in football, music, the Gaelic games in Ireland, Aussie Rules football in Australia etc.

Our Foundation runs a programme called World of Difference which allows people to take a year off work and be paid to work with a charity they really believe in and support. In the UK, this remains totally separate from the Vodafone brand, although it of course has some impact on consumers. But in some countries, such as Romania, we'll treat a programme like this as a sponsorship property and build marketing around it. In some respects, we'd see the traditional domain of corporate responsibility as being open to a sponsorship treatment.

richard crookes

Head of Corporate Brand Management at BASF SE

Richard is Head of Corporate Brand Management at BASF SE, responsible globally for brand strategy development and implementation across all businesses, building a differentiating and relevant brand proposition.

Previously, he was Senior Manager for Allianz SE Brand Communication, developing the Allianz global brand proposition and execution of the first global image campaign which resulted in Allianz entering a major long-term partnership with BMW Williams F1. Richard began his career in advertising at DMB&B working with Procter and Gamble.

When I moved to Allianz, my role was initially to place Allianz in a global context with a corporate advertising campaign. I can't talk in any official capacity about Allianz, so this is entirely personal opinion and memory.

I remember one day I took a call from Williams F1 regarding sponsorship, so we invited them in to see what they had to say. Our perception of sponsoring, at that point, went along familiar lines: you stick a logo on a car, that car travels around the world and a lot of people see the logo - or don't. And that's more or less the way we did it to start. The big learning for me was how the logo on the car is your entry to a world of amazing brand building opportunities.

A lot of companies seem to get stuck. They invest heavily in the platform, but forget the explanation of what that logo actually means in that context. Just because it's stuck on the edge of a football pitch at the World Cup doesn't mean people know who you are, what you do or why they should even care about you.

The best sponsorships demonstrate a credible reason why the brand is involved. What we chose for Allianz at that time was safety. The Allianz Centre for Technology is frequently consulted by the automotive industry to assist with road safety issues. Reducing accidents is not only socially beneficial but commercially important. So safety, at the highest technological level, was demonstrably relevant.

Having a clear positioning around our involvement gave us more reason to talk to the media. Each year we brought out a Safety Dictionary, and produced high quality graphics with Allianz branding to explain the fascination of F1 safety technology, which the media used.

The content you receive as a sponsor is generic, so to drive particular image facets, we produced a TV programme for global broadcast in multiple formats, an F1 lifestyle/technology show. Any animations or footage we generated would carry the Allianz logo, and each show would always contain a particular safety story - the hazards related to specific tracks or conditions - embedding relevant messaging.

a lot of companies… invest heavily in the platform, but forget the explanation of what that logo actually means in that context

Each part of the mix - car branding, spots, bumper branding, content, press - plays a different role, and the value is in having a single global platform.

And all of that comes from the fact that we had a logo on a car!

martin lindstrom

CEO and Chairman of LINDSTROM company, and Chairman of BUYOLOGY INC

Martin is a 'brand futurist', the CEO and Chairman of LINDSTROM company, and Chairman of BUYOLOGY INC, advising companies including Nokia and McDonald's. His brand-building shows attract 800,000 people across the world. He has written five books including 'Buyology'.

In 1994 Martin formed BBDO Interactive Europe, then BBDO Interactive Asia which became the largest internet solution companies in their regions. At thirty, Lindstrom was appointed global COO of British telecom Looksmart.

The vast majority of sponsorship doesn't work because it is aimed at the conscious part of the brain, which neuroscience tells us, accounts for no more than 15% of our cognitive capacity. We are bombarded with thousands of direct marketing messages a day, very few of which we are able to take in, let alone process into changing buying behaviour.

The communications industry spends its time measuring awareness and hoping that some value transfer takes place, something we have never been able to prove. Now we can, and I'm convinced that we will see the sponsorship model change dramatically as a result.

> ### I'm convinced that we will see the sponsorship model change dramatically

Marketing people must realise it is not about plastering your logo everywhere, it is about context, and about embedding the message within the narrative of the story being told, whether that is a football match or a James Bond movie. Our research into this is extensive, and it tells us that when a brand appears in a story at the wrong moment, we don't just ignore it, we delete it from our mind, such is our irritation at being interrupted. Having a logo on the perimeter board is not worth the money. Likewise, rights-holders must prove they are about more than just awareness, which is not so valuable as it was 20 years ago, when the sponsorship model was built that still applies today.

There are so many poor marketing people out there who must now ask themselves, do we have an emotional strategy? Do we have a subconscious strategy? What kind of indirect signals do we want to send?

I'm very impressed by Marlboro's ability to take the core values of Formula One – sex, speed, innovation, coolness - and apply them to a cigarette brand. An amazing achievement. On a personal level I hate it, but professionally there is much to recommend.

We carried out experiments just showing a Formula One car, and people immediately craved cigarettes. What Marlboro have done is create a huge number of what I call submergible components to their brand. They are sending indirect, subconscious signals that are talking to the brain without explicitly telling it we are being sold to.

Sponsorship works when we are not really aware of the signals being sent: the messages get through because our guard is down not up. A Formula One car passing below me with no logo is an example of this, and as a smoker it creates a craving, Pavlovian effect.

When there are logos around, my rational mind tells me I shouldn't crave those things. Without the logo my instinct kicks in and I want to smoke. The evidence is mounting that the most powerful form of sponsorship today is where you do not have a logo but you make up for this with submergible components of the brand.

dany bahar

Commercial & Brand Director of Ferrari S.p.A.

Dany Bahar is Commercial & Brand Director of Ferrari S.p.A. He began his career in finance in Switzerland. He worked for the Fritz Kaiser Group before moving to Red Bull in 2003 where in addition to being given a broad operating canvas by the CEO, he was also appointed a member of the executive management board. Dany has experience in promotion and sponsorship as well as in sales and marketing.

We sell sponsorship, but we certainly don't think of ourselves as a rights-holder. Ferrari is a strong brand, and we don't want to build our business on helping other people to strengthen their brands at our expense. If you look into our collaborations, they all reflect Ferrari's DNA, production values, design, style, attitude and technology. We've always been about manufacturing products and racing so a partnership with Ferrari isn't simply about the logo.

We don't think of our sponsors as sponsors, we think of them as strategic partners. Shell, AMD, Bridgestone, Etihad, Acer: with most of them we have collateral business relationships.

With Shell we started in the 1950's. We celebrated together in 2007 the 60th anniversary of our partnership. They really play a part in our organisation as a technology partner: we have ten Shell engineers working here helping to develop the F1 and road car engines and we promote Shell in our own car marketing brochures. We have more than 25 people in house from Tata Consultancies, helping us become more efficient in road and F1 technology.

Our relationship with Puma is five years old. We have a common understanding and we work very closely. They're a great company to deal with and Puma has become a true strategic partner. They identified F1 as a core business and simply focused on it, whereas adidas and Nike didn't think motor-racing could be a business for them.

Sponsorship has always been a more intelligent way to communicate your brand than simply advertising. Sponsorship gives you a face, it gives brands the opportunity to show customers what they stand for, to deliver reassurance and credibility. How well does Shell stand for high technology fuels without Ferrari? For a consumer, the message is easy to understand because the sponsorship demonstrates Shell competence; the high tech fuel for F1 brings benefits to the end consumer. F1 gives you the impression Shell fuel will do more for your car than the competition, more power. Where is the equivalent visual face for BP?

we sell sponsorship, but we certainly don't think of ourselves as a rights-holder

Sponsorship in general has evolved. In the past, it was just advertising space, and didn't require much analysis, but now it's much tighter in terms of deliverables, more tangible, more professional. I don't believe that sponsorship as simple brand exposure is going to last for much longer. In sport, it's already down to the Olympics, the World Cup, and maybe Euro. And honestly, where's the synergy between a car manufacturer and the Olympics? Sponsorship has to work harder than that.

We choose partners where there's genuine synergy, and we offer them a 360° partnership with Ferrari, a stake in the Ferrari world, in our business. In F1, it's about making participation sustainable. With development costs of £200m each year and £60-70m in sponsorship, who's going to pay the difference?

simon thompson

European Managing Director & Chief Marketing Officer of lastminute.com group

Simon is European Managing Director & Chief Marketing Officer of lastminute.com group, Europe's largest online travel and leisure business. Previously he was Senior Director for Marketing Europe at Motorola, helping generate the greatest level of sales in Motorola's history.

Simon has received numerous Cannes Lions for outstanding creative work and is ranked among the UK's top marketers by Marketing and Campaign magazines. He is also a senior member of the Marketing Society.

There's a world of difference between a sponsorship and a partnership, as defined by a shared commercial goal, whereas sponsorship most of the time, is transference of money from the brand owner to an event or property for a set of rights. It's interesting that when pushed, it takes a while before I can come up with a really great example of sponsorship.

But when Motorola launched a Dolce & Gabbana phone, both brands marketed it through their own channels and it was great for both brands. The partnership came about when Motorola's marketing team were at an event, showing off a new product and the designers from Dolce & Gabbana saw the product, thought it was fantastic and wanted to turn it into their own.

From there on in it became a commercial partnership which was endorsed from the very top of both organisations. The brand strategy of Motorola at that time was to own the fashion phone category, and by partnering with one of the big fashion houses, it was a no-brainer. It got Motorola distribution into high street fashion stores and top end department stores. Let's be honest, Selfridges and a Dolce & Gabbana retail store is a better place to present a high-end fashion product than Carphone Warehouse. And it worked commercially, the new distribution network was incredibly profitable.

The key to a good sponsorship is the correlation between the sponsor and the property, and the selection process is key to this. You have to make sure that the consumer you're aiming at and the audience for the property are exactly the same, and that the brand promise of the event and your product are perfectly aligned. You have to have one very clear objective that both organisations can share. My experience tells me that achieving these aims is difficult, quite often because the chief executive has got the hots for a particular event. The problem for the sponsorship community is that this is how they sell.

To me the media value debate is at best inappropriate. You have to set objectives outside of that. Fundamentally, whatever your target audience, you must have some very clear metrics and you have to take a judgement that it is going to be more effective in achieving these than some of the other channels available. Is it the only way you can get to that target audience?

The challenge for sponsorship is to be seen as a more strategic tool, I think it is still seen on the periphery of the decision-making process, which is fundamentally wrong. The world is multi-channel and the consumer is multi-channel and we have to find the most cost-effective and best way of getting to them.

the problem for the sponsorship community is that this is how they sell

peter wells

Founder of Nilewide

Peter Wells is the founder of Nilewide, providing detailed analysis of key strategic issues as a set of useable tools for marketing practitioners as well as guiding Nilewide's global success in its Australian and London offices. Peter has an MSc in Gene Technology and a Masters in marketing.

As sponsorships become less effective, we're slowly thinking what sponsorship is all about, a dimension which is essence rather than definition.

To me the key to sponsorship is that a sponsor can bring something to consumers which they wouldn't have got otherwise. And by that I mean that, instead of having something forced on them, consumers will have a sense of 'oh, that's pretty cool'. This is quite special because it changes what sponsorship is about. At the highest level it's often hard to see. AIG sponsoring Man U for example.

When you come to other arts and sports events, they only exist because sponsors make it possible. Marketers tend to think of people as consumers but in reality we're individuals active within different social groups, and in reality brands don't have much role within most of that. Sponsorship aligns very clearly with the idea that marketing needs to fit inside people's lives - that the conversations and relationships which matter are people's conversations and relationships with each other, not with a company or a brand. And the unique thing about sponsorship is that it can fit into those areas which are important to consumers.

One of the problems of sponsorship is that it gets confused with advertising. That's the case with rugby when you get 23 ads around the perimeter and that's not sponsorship in any true sense, that's just sales messaging. Sponsors, if they're able to understand, instead of forcing a false relationship between themselves and the customer, can be a small but genuine part of the relationships which matter.

An example of where sponsorship clearly works is where Red Bull will sponsor a big wave quest, bringing something to the group of people interested in people being towed into 30' or 50' waves, as opposed to what Quikripabong sponsor. Or the product placement of an Omega watch, which is just trying to put your brand into something which somebody watches.

> **instead of forcing a false relationship between themselves and the customer, sponsors can be a small but genuine part of the relationships which matter**

I think the idea of rights-holders can hold back what sponsorship is about. The key definition is about bringing something to people for which they're grateful; and what you like and are passionate about doesn't have to be something that somebody else owns. Salomon can sponsor a snowboard park, the real thing is that the kids are having a good time and the really important stuff is what the kids are talking about.

HUTCH MOCEAN CAM

YAMAHA

david butler

Former Marketing Director for Honda Racing Formula 1

David was, until recently, the Marketing Director for Honda Racing Formula 1 where he coordinated Honda's F1 marketing platforms, including Honda's Earth Car initiative. In the sports marketing and media industry for over 17 years, David was previously Marketing Director for Laureus and Head of Laureus Sport for Good Foundation and before that, Divisional Director at Octagon. Whilst in Sydney, he trained as a boxer and is now a trustee of 'Fight for Peace' in Woolwich, East London.

Sport is a universal language, like music, that can break boundaries, unite, create shared experience, harness passions and loyalties.

I've been privileged to meet social sporting entrepreneurs from the edge of the Andes to inner city Melbourne who are using sport to make positive change. It's the stuff that soft drink ads or sports clothes makers couldn't dream of: changing and saving lives.

Inspiring people like Matthew Spacie, whose Magic Bus programme gives homeless children in India a chance to enjoy their birthright: childhood, rather than enslavement in factory labour or worse. And Luke Dowdney in Rio de Janeiro - and now in Woolwich, East London - who created a boxing and educational programme to lure children away from the drugs gangs and a cycle of violence, prison and death. Scotty Lee, who drove the aid convoys to a besieged Sarajevo bereft of penicillin or basic supplies, who now puts his UEFA Coaching Licence to use creating Spirit of Soccer, a soccer programme that teaches children in landmine encrusted Bosnia and Cambodia that the most important thing a footballer needs is not tactical vision but legs. A soccer programme literally saving hundreds of lives through landmine awareness.

And, perhaps most pertinently, two coaches, brought together by a sports and education programme on an orange dustbowl soccer pitch in Sierra Leone: one, whose twin had been shot dead in front of him after his eyes had been burnt out with the bottom of a burning plastic bottle; the other, a part of the rebel troop that killed him; now both teaching tomorrow's generation about reconciliation using a soccer ball on a soccer pitch.

None of the above are charities. As my friend Flavio Pimente, who runs the world famous Meniños do Morumbi programme in São Paolo told me: 'this is my life project and I put everybody inside it.' These are businesses, micro-programmes that when joined together create a hugely powerful force for change; an inspiring marketing and sponsorship programme that literally changes the world and that brands and sponsors should be falling over themselves to engage with.

it's the stuff that soft drink ads or sports clothes makers couldn't dream of: changing and saving lives

While we struggle with the terminology and the proliferation of articles and case studies grows to try and work out whether it's social marketing, CSR, cause-related or something else, inspiring social entrepreneurs are getting on with it and harnessing the true power of sport to change the world – maybe only one soccer pitch at a time, but change it nonetheless.

As sponsorship moves from billboards and athletes to experiential and fans; the evolution continues. We are the lucky 1% of the world's population. Rather than ignore the rest of it, sport is a major catalyst and language that can reach and talk to everybody. Our issue is that we live in a world of many worlds – first and third. Rather than talk to ourselves, sport is one of the things that reminds us that we all live in the same place.

alain de botton

Writer of essayistic books and founder of The School of Life

Alain is a writer of essayistic books, described as a 'philosophy of everyday life'. He's written on love, travel, architecture and literature with bestsellers in 30 countries.

Alain founded The School of Life, dedicated to a new vision of education. He also helps run a production company: Seneca Productions.

Alain gained global recognition with How Proust can change your life.

Some of the most worthwhile of human enterprises don't make money. They are of enormous value to the species, but can't pay their way unaided. We are used to thinking that anything that is really necessary must be capable of being harnessed to a business model, but that simply isn't true. Subsidy is an essential part of so many things we think of as valuable, not least, raising children (the greatest subsidy of all is that which parents give to their kids).

So in principle, sponsorship is both necessary and noble. To sponsor something is to recognise that one has more money than one needs and hoarding it would be immoral when there are so many worthwhile causes out there. Sometimes, people knock sponsors as being interested in their own glory, but how nice that they should in the first place have decided to pin their hopes for glory on noble projects (rather than blowing the money on a party, for example).

I have been consistently sponsored in my life. First, by my parents, then by the state university system, finally, in my working life, at different points, by commercial organisations. I have lost certain publishers quite large sums of money. They would consider the money to have been destroyed in unwise investments. I prefer to think that, semi-consciously, these large corporations did a bit of sponsorship. I have made a number of television programmes with Channel 4. These programmes lost the channel money, but the channel decided to make them anyway, for reasons of prestige, because they believed in the concept more than they believed in generating hard cash.

I take comfort from the way that many of my greatest heroes in literature had sponsors. After all, no one could make a living from selling books until the end of the nineteenth century. Marcel Proust was sponsored by his dad throughout his life. On the one hand, you could think that he was a spoilt dilettante. On the other hand, the few million pounds he cost his father were some of the best spent millions in the history of humanity.

In a time when people love to be pragmatic and hard-headed, let's remember that sponsorship fills vital gaps in our society, between what we really love and what can generate money. Of course sponsors want glory, and want to maximise their brand exposure, but let them: it is their wisdom to seek glamour in the most noble of places. The world will be a sadder planet when the wealthy and large corporations stop wanting to associate themselves with the many important things which don't make any money.

sponsorship is both necessary and noble

philip o'brien

Director of UNICEF's global Private Fundraising and Partnerships Division

Philip is Director of Private Fundraising and Partnerships Division, The United Nations Children's Fund (UNICEF). He has served with UNICEF for 20 years; including as UN Coordinator, Operation Lifeline Sudan in the Southern Sector as well as directly contributing to new programming approaches between UNICEF and the World Bank.

Philip began his career in commercial banking before joining Concern Worldwide, becoming Country Director in Tanzania and Bangladesh, then joining UNICEF as Chief of Health and Nutrition in the Bangladesh Office.

For info on UNICEF Corporate Alliances, contact Jussi Ojutkangas on jojutkangas@unicef.org

About ten years ago, when UNICEF was working with the World Bank in Bangladesh, we spent a while to consider whether our time was best spent lobbying for money to fund our own programmes, or working with the Bank to help it spend its money in ways which were more beneficial for kids. We came to the conclusion to work with the Bank and the outcome was the redesign of some of its programmes, to ensure its support for nutrition extended beyond ensuring people have enough food to include basic health services and opportunities for mothers to obtain greater access to care and support for their kids.

Partnership isn't always about fundraising. In our case, more and more, it's about what's best for kids and that's a mindset change we're still driving. We've invested in the capabilities to manage these relationships, to help us go round to the other side of the table to see what's in it for our partners. There has to be a recognition that we both see the world through different eyes, but, providing you have a partner who is genuinely interested in your work, there is usually a meeting place.

> *partnership isn't always about fundraising. In our case, more and more, it's about what's best for kids*

Our partnership with Pampers is not without its critics. The audience fit is perfect and the relationship has delivered very tangible benefits for both parties, including raising more than 150 million vaccines to protect mothers and babies against tetanus, but as an organisation with an international membership, scope and presence, our members question whether they really want to see UNICEF associated with cause-related marketing. So, although there's more that we could explore with P&G, we're still evaluating the impact on our brand equity.

With Barcelona's membership-based ownership structure, it was an instinctive fit for UNICEF, as we didn't have to worry about issues of commercialisation. And with the previous Chairman's desire to position Barcelona as 'more than just a club', we offered them the 'more' he was looking for - a well known global brand, highly respected in Spain, with a mandate that is unequalled.

The word sponsorship is not one we would find in our lexicon. It has its own sector-specific meaning, but sponsorship also suggests a degree of control, by the sponsor, which we couldn't allow. UNICEF is driven by a set of ethical principles to protect the rights of children. We need to maintain our impartiality and independence at all times and so do not endorse any company, product or service.

andy walsh

General Manager of FC United of Manchester

Andy is General Manager of FC United of Manchester, a fan-owned football club formed by disenchanted and disenfranchised Manchester United fans. The club has over 2,000 members and has won successive promotions.

Andy is a fervent campaigner for fan involvement in football clubs. As Chair of the Independent Manchester United Supporters' Association, he led the successful campaign to stop the takeover of Manchester United by BSkyB.

Football fans tend to have an uneasy relationship with sponsors, who tend to be an easy target for their discontent. This is unfortunate because in many cases clubs, or whole sports, would not exist if it weren't for the money sponsors provide.

But I have a problem when commercial interests overtake those of the organisation and its supporters, which is sadly all too often the case. It's how the revenues are used that causes me the greatest concern because often they're used just to line the pockets of a few people running the clubs or leagues. That's not the fault of sponsors, it's the fault of those who are charged with looking after the long-term future of the game. I don't blame the corporate sector, I blame those running the sport.

Football sponsorship money should be used for team building, community work and to subsidise entry prices to make sure the sport remains accessible to as wide an audience as possible. The escalating ticket prices show that this isn't the case, and there is a resentment from some supporters toward people who know little about their sport obtaining tickets from corporate sponsors, while those people who've supported the sport over many years are left outside. That resentment tends to fester.

Corporate sponsors want to be part of the passion and atmosphere that is generated by a crowd at a football match. But if you cram the stadium full of corporate visitors and squeeze out the ordinary supporters, that passion is lost. That balance needs to be redressed. I've been to away games with Manchester United when many of the people standing around me know very little about the team or the players.

The passion of the crowd has also diminished because younger people who generate a lot of the atmosphere can't afford to get in. The average age of a fan in the Premier League is around 42. That is not good for the future of the game. We talk a lot about the corporatisation of the game and we are critical of the suits who turn up at matches; you go along to a football match to be involved in the atmosphere and to contribute to it, not just stand there and absorb it.

What has happened since the advent of the Premier League is that football has been taken further and further up-market, deliberately so. It was the marketing strategy of the Premier League in their Blueprint for Football report, to take the game to people with the greater disposable income, and to socially engineer out those people they thought were more trouble than they were worth. And they are the same people who are creating atmosphere in the stadium. To many fans, sponsors are the public face of that strategy.

football sponsorship money should be used for team building, community work and to subsidise entry prices

lesa ukman

Chairman and CEO of Altis marketing LLC

Lesa is the co-founder of IEG. She works directly with sponsor and property clients of IEG's Advisory Services and Research groups and is IEG's primary product development director, also responsible for the content and focus of IEG's Annual Sponsorship Conference.

Prior to establishing IEG with her brother Jon Ukman, she worked in the Mayor's Office of Special Events for the City of Chicago. In 2000 she was inducted into the International Festivals & Events Association/Miller Brewing Company Hall of Fame.

My first job after college was in the Mayor's office in Chicago, helping deliver campaign promises, which included backing for the Chicago Blues Festival. But the money ran out so I began to ring corporations to ask for their support and fell in love with the idea of sponsorship – as a way for companies to do good, do good business and make cities better. The social side of sponsorship has always been a hook for me but it's really about whatever the public loves. A football team in the UK, an elephant festival in Thailand – the type of property is irrelevant.

At the end of the day, it's about connecting with people emotionally. If you can enhance what people care about, make the experience better, different, more accessible, the halo you earn takes you into different territory, an emotional territory where a name on a signboard is not going to take you. For 20 years the NFL and FIFA have been asking to come and talk at the conference - but what do they really have to teach?

Sponsorship needs to get out from the narrow perspective of marketing departments. The idea of doing sponsorship for something bigger is what excites me. I always regret we never managed to get Anita Roddick over to our conference because she was a visionary and built campaigning into the DNA of the brand. And led the way for brands like Ben and Jerry's and Patagonia.

Red Bull is another success brand, built on a DNA of action sports and entertainment. Dietrich Mateschitz really recognises that sponsorship is more than marketing. It wasn't, 'We're going to do this for three months'; it was, 'This is what we are as a company and we're embedding this into our brand'. You don't see this often in big companies because they're all run by committees. It's not that it can't happen, but you need such a big visionary.

Action sports have done a lot of interesting things - when you're so niche, you have to be creative. Motorola partnered with Burton and they created a co-branded line of snowboard jackets, pre-wired for mobile phones to make it easy to use on the slopes. It was never going to be a business model - but what it did for Motorola was take their brand into snowboard and surf stores, not as a commodity but as an insider. It took their business to a different place.

sponsorship needs to get out from the narrow perspective of marketing departments

marc gobé

President of Emotional Branding LLC, designer, photographer, filmmaker and author

Designer, photographer, filmmaker, respected author and sought-after public speaker Marc Gobé focuses on connecting brands emotionally with people.

He is President of Emotional Branding LLC, an experimental think tank with clients like Unilever; he's also Co-Founder and former Co-President of Desgrippes Gobé worldwide.

Marc champions the role of design and creative collaboration in successful brand innovation that taps into human emotion, and has twice been elected one of the most influential designers in retail by DDI magazine.

Our world is turning upside down. From a consumer perspective the Babyboomers, whose generation influenced everything we have known for the past 40 years, are being replaced by Gen X and Y, who just don't look at the world or brands the same way as the well-off shopping -hungry Babyboomers.

The consumer-driven economy is being replaced by a values-driven one and the way people spend their money will change fundamentally. People are concerned about their environment, tired of obtrusive advertising and want to relate to brands that are trustworthy. In short they want a 'real' emotional connection.

A shining example of what I mean is the communication platform and brand-building by the Barack Obama presidential campaign, which reached out to the hearts of the American people – a grassroots movement linked to a powerful web-driven integration of different media.

The web will become the primal force in marketing, and communities will form around common needs, and new sets of shared values. Running in parallel to this trend is the end of the era of big advertising budgets, and communication in general will be less intrusive and more respectful of people's privacy and intelligence. The task of today's marketers is to create products that surprise, entertain and appeal to the senses. My belief is that products that are welcomed in people's lives are what makes advertising work - not the other way around. This elevates products from commodity status to being able to stimulate people's emotions – and build brands faster and more cost-effectively.

Sponsors exist in a new environment, where time is more valuable than money, people acquire fewer material goods and prefer to live better lives. Cause marketing is not just a logo on a charity event, it means brands having to stand for something bigger. These emotional trends are the most potent ideas in branding today and define how we have to see marketing: through the eyes of people in a consumer democracy. Emotional Branding is about doing more with less by humanising brands, predicting the end of the consumer world as we know it and encouraging brands to be truthful and responsible.

cause marketing is not just a logo on a charity event, it means brands having to stand for something bigger

But the signs are that there is a long way to go. The advertising and sponsorship industry is still stuck in 'more is better', pushing unwanted messages and silly guerilla tactics. Sponsorship can surely be more than Pepsi trying to own the Obama inauguration, a tactic that failed and disgusted people.

I am always amazed by how much people love brands and how much the branding industry is so out of step with the emotional reality of the marketplace. Time to step up for gen 'xY' in a new emotional economy.

CHANGE
WE NEED

www.BARACKOBAMA.COM

PAID FOR BY OBAMA FOR AMERICA

Courtesy of Brooke Medlin

dave stewart

singer, songwriter, producer, creative

Dave has achieved over 75 million album sales as one half of the Eurythmics with Annie Lennox, honoured in 1999 with a Lifetime Achievement Award at the Brits. He is renowned for his huge contribution to charity through music, including staging the Nelson Mandela AIDS concert that went live to over a billion people. With Microsoft co-founder Paul Allen, Dave created 'The Hospital', a multi media creative centre. He also set up the media company 'Weapons of Mass Entertainment' and, in 2008, was made Advisor to Nokia.

Annie and I never accepted any sponsorship through our career, but that was a different time. At that moment we were kind of naïve and wanted to keep our songs and performances and everything in the purest form, so you didn't see brands slapped across our performances, Pepsi above our heads, as we did 'Don't mess with the missionary man', say.

As I went into the 90s, I realised more and more that we might as well be accepting sponsorship because the big record companies are just like any other business, like sponsors, but the worst ones because they take all your rights. When it comes to sponsorship, say by a brand like Burberry, as an artist, why isn't that as cool as being sponsored by EMI, when EMI make everything from school clothing to sonic radar systems?

So when I started to explore the parameters of how the entertainment industry works, I understood very quickly that the web was going to break the old model, totally, not just music, but the entire way business works.

There are a million people running around claiming they've got the 'new way' but there isn't a 'new way'. Everyone keeps thinking that the future is standing still, in one place like, but it's liquid. You can't write a business model for it.

My little business creates anything from mobile games to TV shows to music and distributes it in completely novel ways; which creates another model for how people can do it. We're launching a mobile game soon with Nokia, with music by a completely new artist, on 30 million cellphones. Advertising and sponsorship are integral to this new model. I've got a few powerful ideas about the future of advertising or sponsorship. In fact, I created a word – sponsor-bility. So you go to a little fish 'n' chip shop, and say to them 'Do you realise you have sponsor-bility? You're paying £12K a year in advertising in your local paper and you could have sponsored the download of the new album by Errors and become the most famous fish 'n' chip shop in the world'.

Nylon magazine has just taken on the Plasti-scines, a Parisian group. 21 year old girls from Paris – they sound like a rock band but dress in great stuff. It's a blurry line because Nylon's releasing a record under their own label, but it's a great fit, they're benefiting equally and that's the idea behind sponsorship.

> **you pay £12k pa advertising in your local paper - for the same money you could sponsor the download of the new album by Errors and become the most famous fish 'n' chip shop in the world**

gang of

david aaker

Vice Chairman of Prophet

David A. Aaker is Vice-Chairman of Prophet (www. prophet.com), Professor Emeritus the Haas School of Business, UC Berkeley, and executive advisor to Dentsu. Named as one of the top five most important marketing/ business gurus in 2007, he is a recognised authority on brand strategy having won three career awards for contributions to the science of marketing. He has published over 100 articles and 14 books translated into 18 languages including his latest, 'Spanning Silos: the New CMO Imperative.'

Sponsorship offers unique advantages in brand building.

Whereas advertising is intrusive and is clearly a paid message overtly attempting to persuade or change attitudes, a sponsorship can become part of people's lives. Advertising is good at communicating attributes and functional benefits. Yet most strong brands go beyond to provide emotional and self-expressive benefits, to have a personality, and to differentiate on intangible attributes. Sponsorship can be very effective at extending brands beyond attributes since they develop associations that add depth, richness and a contemporary feel to the brand and the brand-customer relationship.

The primary goal of a sponsorship is usually to create exposure for the brand and to develop associations. However, there are four other brand-building benefits that can be very relevant to the selection and evaluation of sponsorships. A sponsorship can mobilise the organisation for brand building, particularly one that has difficulty spanning organisational silos and provide an event experience to customers connecting the brand to the event/customer bond. It also provides the opportunity for firm executives to interact in a social relationship with those affecting their business, such as retail executives.

> **sponsorship can develop associations that add depth, richness and a contemporary feel to the brand and the brand-customer relationship**

But perhaps the most significant thing that sponsorship can do is inject energy into the brand, We can define this in several ways: involvement with the customer, how interesting you are and how much buzz you create. If you make a boring product like insurance, nobody is going to talk about you, so the opportunity is to attach your brand with something that has this buzz, a World Cup or an Olympics for example.

The problem for sponsors is that there is a shortage of good events with which to associate, so creating their own makes good sense if you can do it well. It means you don't raise the fees every year and can ensure that the event fits perfectly with your other marketing programmes. The Avon Walk for Breast Cancer is an interesting example. Although it is organised by the Avon Foundation and supported by Reebok and Genetech, it has carried the Avon brand for 18 years, raised $550 million for breast cancer research, and continues to grow.

Successful sponsorships, such as VISA's sponsorship of the Olympics, have a long term horizon, measured in decades instead of years. It takes time to build up an association and leverage that association. The biggest failure in sponsorship is to view it as a short term, one-shot relationship with a property. The sponsorship should become part of the brand's narrative and reflect its core values.

sally hancock

Director of London 2012 partnership and Group Sponsorship for Lloyds TSB

Sally is Director of London 2012 partnership and Group Sponsorship for Lloyds TSB.

Previously, Sally was the founder and Chief Executive of Redmandarin, the international sponsorship consultancy company considered thought leaders in sponsorship; whose clients include Philips, Sony Ericsson and SABMiller. Previously, Sally was VP Strategic Planning at Octagon.

The Race for Life, for Cancer Research UK, is an incredibly strong property for its sponsors. It's established itself as the premium running event for women and is absolutely grounded in issues that affect women. There is nothing quite like it: as a charitable event that raises awareness of the issues, the charity itself and its partners, it's excellent.

Linked to this, I was always very impressed with the work of Avon Cosmetics related to Breakthrough Breast Cancer. For a long time they were tied up with Fashion Targets Breast Cancer which was a really clever way of getting a non-retail cosmetics brand into retail, raising huge sums of money and enabling a dialogue between the brand and women. For an activity that from a rights point of view was relatively low-cost, the benefit to Avon was huge, as it was to the charity. It was a good model of a proper partnership. It identified an issue that affects thousands of women and was done in a sympathetic and appropriate way.

It demonstrated one of the truisms of sponsorship, which is to identify the things that are of passionate interest to your customer base. There are an awful lot of sponsorships which are entirely misdirected when women are the target audience. This is a problem, and an opportunity. A huge proportion of sponsorship is directed at men. Yet from a consumer point of view that doesn't make sense. It may be that women are more accommodating of above the line messages, but I think we could be far cleverer in the way we use sponsorship to reach a female audience.

We make ridiculous assumptions as an industry about the ability of sport to reach women. Clever sponsorship activity looks at things that matter to women and does it in an appropriate way. Quite often the message we get back from research into this, says: 'do something that benefits my kids or do something that benefits the community in which they live'.

Often these things are over-commercialised and we turn off from those messages very quickly. It's wrong to commercialise that emotion but without the commercial partners they couldn't have made it work in the same way, and it wouldn't raise the sums it does for Cancer Research. But it's the emotional power I see coming from the Race of Life that makes it special. I haven't seen it in many other sponsorships.

there are an awful lot of sponsorships which are entirely misdirected when women are the target audience

giles gibbons

Founding partner and CEO of Good Business

Giles is a founding partner and CEO of Good Business, one of Europe's leading Corporate Responsibility Consultancies. Giles started at Cadbury Schweppes, before moving to Saatchi & Saatchi, managing domestic and international marketing campaigns as well as helping create M&C Saatchi in 1995. He then started Good Business with Steve Hilton, advising companies including McDonalds and Coca-Cola. He also co-authored 'Good Business – Your World Needs You'.

Corporate responsibility in its current form has not seen a downturn of the sort we are about to experience, and my sense is that this will put a spotlight on much of the pretty sloppy thinking that currently sits under the CR umbrella. As in other areas of business, the economic downturn will push corporate responsibility into focusing on those things that really matter.

Society as a whole is looking to business to be more responsible, but what this means has changed. It used to mean giving the money to a charity to do something on your behalf, which was a nice thing to do, but on big issues like climate change companies need to be responsible themselves rather than just handing money over to a third party. For this reason CR sponsorship hasn't actually grown as quickly as it might have in the last five years, even though the need to be more responsible has grown a great deal.

As organisations start to get their head around managing their core responsibility, growing it strategically and profitably, then there might be a new opportunity for the sponsorship of charitable and social amenities.

But simply putting your logo onto something feels incredibly unsophisticated now, and is seen through by most consumers. If you really want to gain engagement and support you need to go so much further and offer much more experiential activation around your sponsorship. The old, inevitable question relating to sponsorship is how many eyeballs are on your logo. The vast majority of charity or social responsibility properties cannot match sport in terms of the mass audience it delivers, for example, a UEFA Champions League. But what it can deliver is a much stronger value-driven engagement of targeted individuals, so the experience it offers is a much deeper one.

companies must take that further step and question what it is we really need sponsorship to do

I would class the London Marathon as a social sponsorship rather than a sporting one. Compare how engaged the runners and their families are with the event sponsor Flora, and now Virgin. It's a hell of a lot deeper in terms of the relationship between a brand and its audience, than if they are simply seeing Ford branding at the Champions League.

Now more than ever, companies must take that further step and question what it is we really need sponsorship to do. The answer is often not those things that cost millions and millions of pounds, but those that provide a deeper relationship with the consumer.

prof. simon chadwick

Chair in Sport Business Strategy & Marketing at Coventry University, Director of CIBS.

Professor Simon Chadwick is Chair in Sport Business Strategy and Marketing at Coventry University, where he is also Director of CIBS. At Leeds University Chadwick gained a PhD in sponsorship in football. He is now the world's first professor in sport business strategy.

His research interests are based around sport marketing and sport business strategy and he has published almost 600 books, papers, articles and reports on sport and marketing.

When I was young I had three great passions: football, motorsport and cycling. I would read countless magazines and watch as much television as I could in order to catch a glimpse of the latest race or game. As a result, I was constantly exposed to a flow of seemingly exotic names, colours and images about which I knew absolutely nothing: Haribo, Carrera, Ariston, Systeme U, Brembo, Ceramica Ragno and Belga are just some of the hundreds of names that I could probably recall without too much fuss. I never bought the products - I never actually knew what the products were! - but my brand recall was exceptional. It still is today. Hence, when I had a son of my own, who would ask me to buy sweets for him, I instantly recognised Haribo: sponsors of Giles Villeneuve during his heyday at Ferrari in the late 1970s and early 1980s. The question is, is the durability of my brand recall, and the length of time before my ultimate purchase of a Haribo product, typical or not? Irrespective of the answer, it says something about the power of sponsorship.

But now sponsorship faces some big challenges to the way in which it has traditionally functioned. The rise of new media and social networking are changing how people relate to one another, and to the marketing communications messages they are exposed to everyday. At the same time, as product consumption becomes ever more homogeneous, people are seeking exciting, sometimes risky ways through which they can add 'buzz' to what they buy, eat, drink or wear. This need is, to an extent, bound up in the desire of increasing numbers to enjoy the 'experience' of consumption, rather than merely the con-

sumption itself. For organisations, this means understanding how to create a sense of community, identity and association amongst often highly disparate individuals who may be spread across large geographic areas.

The problem is, while data and digital marketers forge ahead, many sponsors seem still to be stuck in the slow lane and too many still have a transaction mentality: pay-for-the-space; place the logo. However, there is evidence that some sponsors are starting to think in a new way using it as a form of relationship marketing. The future growth of sponsorship may rely on whether sponsors can become social networkers in their own right, can be one of the techno-savvy crowd, and can provide experiences that will never be forgotten by consumers.

Can they truly engage with their customers such that these people become brand ambassadors through their actions as well as through their words? We shall see.

> **the future growth of sponsorship may rely on whether sponsors can become social networkers in their own right**

mark earls

HERDmeister

Mark is a recovering adperson who now writes and talks and works independently under the banner of HERD Consulting, helping people and organisations and their collaborators come to terms with our social or HERD nature.

His latest book 'HERD' has won much applause, being described 'like Malcolm Gladwell on Speed' and 'an essential guide to the new media landscape'. Prior to HERD Mark held senior positions at Ogilvy Group Worldwide and the radical creative co-operative St Luke's.

When I first visited Olafur Eliasson's The Weather Project at London's Tate Modern back in 2003, I remember thinking how delighted the artist must be to have so many people engaging so directly in the experience of his art - one small child next to me insisted on taking his clothes off, so convinced was he that he and his family were now on some sun-drenched beach. But I suspect that the sponsors of the series, Unilever, were even more delighted: their long-running support of commissions for the huge space of the Turbine hall has been an excellent example of how sponsorship might evolve into a more powerful tool in the next few years.

First, it illustrates how sponsorship can work inside and outside the company: it's not merely a matter of the board inviting a few investors and advisors to the opening and then hoping that the public will be grateful for the patronage. Indeed, the efforts by Unilever to use the investment as a springboard for a massive internal cultural change have been rightly rewarded by the Arts sponsorship world.

Second, it demonstrates how sponsorship can be so much more than 'badging', 'association-building' or 'messaging': The Unilever Series provides what leading-edge marketers are calling a 'social object'. That is, something around which people can interact with each other - which is what people really want to do, rather than interact with brands and businesses. Most tellingly, the Series enhances our interactions with each other through the quality of the content and the ingenuity of its presentation. Who can forget Carsten Höller's slides from '06/7 and the glee with which humans of all ages flopped out of the bottom, having experienced what the artist calls their own personal 'inner spectacle'.

Third, it's clear there is no short-term opportunism behind the plan: this has been a significant commitment over many years, with many different artists, so many participating visitors and so many Unilever staff members interacting with each other.

The future of marketing is not about doing things to people, but about providing means for them to interact with each other: to create experiences and interactions that touch their fundamentally social or 'HERD' selves. Sponsorship can and - I believe - should be a big part of this but to do so it has to drop the cliché and rights-obsession that dominates current discussions and recognise that to be effective the sponsor has to do more than badge stuff.

> **the Unilever Series provides what leading edge marketers are calling a 'social object', that is, something around which people can interact with each other**

norman jay mbe

DJ

Norman is one of Britain's most celebrated DJs; the first DJ to receive an MBE for 'services to music and DJ'ing'. He was DJ at the Obama Inauguration parties and the official tour for the late James Brown.

Norman's credits include Mick Jagger's 50th birthday party and the Big Chill 10th anniversary and he returns every year to head up the Good Times party at the Notting Hill Carnival, recently celebrating his 25th anniversary there.

The first thing to say is no organised entertainment can exist without the corporate dollar, and anyone who thinks otherwise is an idiot. That doesn't mean you have to relinquish creative control, or sell your integrity.

There are relationships to be had with the right brand, which allows you to grow creatively. My memories of working with Budweiser was that here were some fantastic people who gave us complete creative freedom, a term which is often misunderstood by brands, who think you are being precious, but as an artist you can never compromise on that.

We have a firmly established brand name of our own, Good Times, and each year play a big free gig at the Notting Hill Carnival, which attracts a lot of young trendy advertising types who are there in their own time and who get it on a fundamental level. But then they have to go back to the office and sell the idea to their clients, who tend to be more conservative.

The risk is that when something goes wrong at the carnival, which is a free event attracting thousands of people, it often gets used by the powers that be to denigrate the whole thing, for their own political reasons. Unlike a sports event we have no control over the bigger picture. What we do have is a democratic and popular event hitting a demographic of opinion formers and fashionistas.

On top of this there is the personal endorsement route – we live in the era of the superstar DJ, who can take a sponsor from MixMag to the Sunday Times magazine and generate great,

original content that can be used across all forms of media: for example our film and music shows have for many years been played on Virgin Atlantic flights. When Sony launched its Vaio laptops, they came to us for blogs and podcasts and all that stuff.

We are not asking for something for nothing but a culture of mutual respect. 'You're a beer company, I won't tell you how to sell your beer so don't tell me how to run my Carnival!' In the States corporate money doesn't go into dance music, full stop. When it does, it's a beer company saying, 'here's a few crates' which is not my idea of sponsorship – I'm a teetotaler for one thing.

we are not asking for something for nothing but a culture of mutual respect

There is a worrying perception I'm picking up that dance music has had its day as a commercial property and that brands are moving on to something else. This could be devastating as most events are small and without a sponsor they won't take place, it is as stark as that. Added to the economic conditions we're facing means we could be pissing in the wind.

patric verrone

Television writer, attorney, and President of the Writers Guild of America, West

Patric is a television writer, attorney, and President of the Writers Guild of America, West. In 2008 he led the successful writers strike over internet writing contracts that attracted worldwide attention.

Over 22 years, Patric has written for hit shows including The Tonight Show and Futurama. He has won two Emmys as well as being listed 75th in Time Magazine's 2008 'Most Influential People in the World'.

For as long as television has existed, it has survived as a medium based on advertiser support and sponsorship. From the days of Texaco Star Theater through a lifetime of 30 second ad spots to season premieres of TV shows presented 'commercial free' by a single sponsor, television has relied on advertising revenue to produce and distribute entertainment and information.

Recently, the television industry has developed a new form of promotion. It involves the incorporation of products into the storytelling, characters, and dialogue of the programming itself. It goes by several names including 'Branded Entertainment', 'Embedded Advertising', and 'Product Integration'. It is necessary to distinguish between traditional product placement and product integration. Product placement is the use of real commercial products as props on a TV show to add authenticity. Product integration takes product placement to a new level by accepting payment to weave commercial products into the storylines, character arcs, and even jokes in a TV show.

It is one thing to have a certain brand of bottled water on the kitchen table as the sitcom family talks about junior's special problem this week. It is something altogether different to make the writers write and the actors act scripted lines that extol the crisp refreshing goodness of that water and to convince the wacky next door neighbor, who happens to be a professional water salesman in this episode, to stock and sell the product.

There is a commonly held belief that there is a business need for product integration. Viewers are using technology to speed through and get away from commercials. So producers and the networks are resorting to other means to give viewers what they clearly are trying to get away from. And they are using writers and actors to do it.

This has become an issue of artistic integrity. Like most writers, I don't use lavender-scented body wash with lanolin, and I don't want to be forced to write it into a script to help sell it. Yet TV networks are forcing writers to incorporate cars, power tools, potato chips, soda, and body wash into scripts. Similarly, actors on these shows have become pitchmen for these products whether they want to be publicly associated with them, whether they've been paid for such a commercial endorsement, and whether they have conflicting relationships with competing brands.

> **like most writers, I don't use lavender-scented body wash with lanolin, and I don't want to be forced to write it into a script to help sell it**

Product integration is more than a concern for writers and actors. It is also a concern for the public. Integrating commercials into shows has created a form of stealth advertising, fooling the viewer into thinking they are not watching an ad. Can the television medium survive sitcommercials and dramertisements? There is a limit to audience willingness to be 'sold to'. Viewers flocking to new media (through internet streaming and downloads) seem very willing to reject production integration and to literally 'pull the plug'.

malcom gerrie

Founder and CEO of Whizz Kid Entertainment

Malcolm is founder and CEO of Whizz Kid Entertainment, a progressive multi-media production company specialising in entertainment and event programming.

Malcolm's early credits include The Tube, The White Room and The Three Tenors. He was also the creative drive behind Initial producing The Brit Awards and The Orange BAFTAs.

Malcolm pioneered advertiser -funded programming and in 2000 he was inducted onto The Music Manager's Forum British Music Roll of Honour.

In terms of sponsor-funded programming, we're all working in a fast changing environment where the regulations are moving to accommodate the objectives of brands. There is no question that this is the way it must go.

The model is becoming increasingly sophisticated, and the television programme is often just the shop window, with the engine being its mobile and online platforms. The secret of a good marriage between the brand and a television programme is to get as accurate as possible a brief from the brand itself, not the agencies. There must be no dilution of the basic idea before the producer gets involved.

My experience has been that the brand lets you get on with it, almost without exception. As long as the idea is good at the beginning and you involve them in some of the bigger decisions and ground rules are established in terms of who has creative control.

The threat to editorial control is one of perception rather than reality, and the criticism of branded content usually comes from an old-fashioned point of view that says, if you get into bed with a brand it's going to assume control of the relationship and what you put on the screen. But that's like saying that if you buy a certain type of motor car it will force you to drive in a certain way. No it doesn't.

In fact, brands can really help editorially as they bring a huge amount of power to the table. Clients such as Nokia for example, carry enormous clout in the music business. Editorially I can get a better product because I get better talent. If I ring Sting or Take That or Girls Aloud and am able to say that not only are they going to be on Channel 4, but also on 1 billion handsets worldwide, it's a potent argument.

My abiding memory of sponsorship is of the Brit Awards, sponsored by MasterCard. We had Michael Jackson flying into the UK to do a one off live performance with a cast of thousands, performing Earth Song at Earls Court. MasterCard flew in all of their senior executives with the big clients they wanted to impress. What happens? Jarvis Cocker decides to jump out of the crowd and invade the stage, gets locked up by the police and it makes the front page of every newspaper in the world the next day.

Imagine the conversation had with the sponsor the following day. At first everybody was freaked but once they put it into perspective and calmed down, they realised they were involved in television history in the making, nobody got hurt and by the way have you seen the ratings? The clients went from very wrinkled brows to big smiles within the space of 24 hours.

the criticism of branded content usually comes from an old-fashioned point of view

nic couchman

Co-founder and Senior Partner of Couchman and Harrington Associates

Nic is co-founder and Senior Partner of Couchman and Harrington Associates, regarded as the leading specialist sports law practice in the country. Nic began a sports law apprenticeship at Townleys, going on to become a partner and Head of Intellectual Property, with clients including the IOC and Coca-Cola. Nic has developed a particular interest in the image rights of sports personalities and pioneered this developing area, working with Wayne Rooney and the World Pro Surfers association.

The rise of player power has been driven in part by sponsors: people relate to people, not institutions, and sponsor brands increasingly understand this. Signage and hospitality are, comparatively, dull, boring and these days ubiquitous. Sponsors need to bring their association with events to life by using the heroes of the sport. This in turn has brought greater recognition of an individual's commercial power.

Stars of golf and tennis have always had to understand their own commercial rights because they were essentially freelance, self-employed people who were free agents to a large extent. But the whole concept of player power has now moved into team sports in a very significant way.

From a legal point of view the question has been: who owns or controls the players' 'image right' - the institution or the individual? That is a struggle that will go on for some time.

Twenty years ago the football club told the player what to do, a master - servant relationship that has changed fundamentally. Laws supporting free agency have proliferated and players have generally become more tuned in to what their commercial potential and entitlements might be.

The development of image rights was in part a response to the influx of European players into the Premier League. In France, Germany, Italy and Spain there has always been a greater legal recognition of the right of an individual to control the commercial exploitation of their personality.

England just happens to have the most powerful league in the world but the UK is just one small market. Two thirds of the players, many of the club owners and managers and the majority of the audience is foreign, and a substantial amount of global media revenue comes from overseas. That fact is key to understanding the notion of player power in football. These players are global stars, on posters and television programmes in Malaysia, Singapore or India, selling product in countries thousands of miles away.

But without institutions such as leagues and clubs and without matches to participate in, supported by broadcasters, they wouldn't have that platform, that market.

It is not just in the multi-billion dollar global soccer market where the talent is making its commercial presence felt. A particular interest of mine is pro surfing, where the top athletes are waking up to their commercial potential as a collective, and have formed their own entirely athlete-owned association, the World Pro Surfers, to create and implement group sponsorship initiatives.

Sport has been a fully-fledged business for only twenty five years or so and it is rather early to judge if the rise in player power has 'peaked' or will continue its upward trajectory. The growth of celebrity culture generally shows no sign of abating, however, and the global soap opera of sport continues to produce its heroes and villains. It is a reasonable bet that player power still has a long way to go.

people relate to people, not institutions

wayne **rabbit** bartholomew

1978 World Champion Surfer and former President of the Association of Surf Professionals

Rabbit's journey in surfing began in 1967. Crowned World Champion in 1978, he placed top five for eight consecutive years and came within a whisker of regaining the title in 1983. Rabbit's biography, Bustin down the door, tells the story of the birth of pro' surfing; and was turned into a cinematic documentary in 2008. Rabbit recently resigned as President of the Association of Surf Professionals, a position he held for ten years, to develop a new environmental business venture.

Surfing has never done very well in terms of non endemic sponsors. A lot of the corporate world still doesn't get it because they don't walk the talk – and, if you don't surf, it's nearly impossible to get surfing. They still see surfing as Gidget and the Beach Boys. A lot of corporates use surf imagery, but if you brand something badly, it's so clear to surfers that it's phoney, and next minute there's a rejection. And you could say the surf industry's shunned the outside world as well. They don't take to non endemics very well.

If a big whale turned up and threw $10m at the ASP, I'm sure it would be taken seriously. But with $2-3m, it wouldn't. The surf brands don't like the fit with brands they see as totally uncool, they see it as a dilution of their brand value. And they dominate in so many categories, there's not a lot they don't make now.

For me personally the surf industry was like a cottage industry in the 70s, and my experience wasn't that great. The rules were quite primitive, for example, you had to wear different shorts for each contest. At Pipeline you'd wear Offshore, in Hawaii OP, a hopeless situation for personal sponsorship. I'd get fined $1000 at every event for wearing my own sponsor's shorts. And in those days, you had to finish 3rd in a world series event just to win $1200. This went on for years.

So I was World Champion and barely getting by. None of my generation made any money. Then Tom Carroll and Tom Curren walked in with million dollar contracts and if I finished in the top five for eight years nowadays, I'd be worth tens of millions. But we had the satisfaction of laying the foundation for what pro surfing is today. We were paid no money, but we got to ride on un-crowded waves.

if you brand something badly, it's so clear to surfers that it's phoney, and next minute there's a rejection

My first clear impression of sponsorship was in 1978. I had a manager, Ken Brown, and we ended up securing one of the first non surf industry sponsorships with Smirnoff. The deal was worth $20K and I had to go round the world in a white suit - the man in white was their image. And I remember one board meeting in Sydney, standing in front of them to pitch. Surfing certainly didn't have an image conducive to sponsorship at the time. So this gentleman said to me, my son plays rugby in the winter and he's a surf lifeguard in the summer. Why should we give money to you, a surfer? That made me realise exactly what we were facing.

For me personally, Nike is by far the most successful sponsor - Tiger Woods, Roger Federer, all the big names of international sport, starting with Michael Jordan. It's amazing how they do it.

ross rebagliati

Director of Snowboard and Ski Operations for the resort Kelowna Mountain

Ross is Director of Snowboard and Ski Operations for the resort Kelowna Mountain in British Columbia. He is also the founder of the Rebagliati Alpine Snowboard Training Academy – where students receive World Cup standard training.

A professional snowboarder, Ross' wins include the 1996 World Cup; at the 1998 Winter Olympics Ross won the first ever gold medal for snowboarding. In 2005 he was inducted into the British Columbia Sports Hall of Fame.

Snowboarding was under the radar until it was accepted into the 1998 Olympics in Nagano, Japan. Up until that point it was the wild west. From a sponsorship point of view a few board companies would give you free stuff, but there wasn't the corporate culture that has grown up around the sport today.

As athletes, all we wanted was to get a sponsor who would pay for us to be able to travel and compete, but unless you were in the top five in the world, you'd be lucky to find any company who would talk to you. Most of my personal sponsors were European because 90% of the World Cup Circuit took place in Europe. The sponsor who really helped me was F2, they saw how potentially significant the sport was becoming before many of the others. In Europe snowboarding was accepted much more readily than it was in North America, and even then the freestyle side of the sport brought in more money than the racing. The take-up of computer games really pushed the freestyle guys' profiles, with Tony Hawk leading the way.

Now I'm 38 years old, I'm in the market to buy a Porsche or a Rolex. All these young kids who grew up snowboarding and skateboarding have got kids now, and we're the ones buying the BMWs, mutual funds, pensions or real estate.

After I won the Olympic gold medal I got some bigger corporate sponsors but the controversy surrounding my being stripped of the gold snuffed them out fairly quick. I tested positive for marijuana, but it was second-hand smoke. This whole controversy came up for no reason at all, I didn't break any rules.

I hated the fact that the relationships I'd built up over a long period of time - and in their minds they were taking a risk on an extreme sports athlete - disintegrated within minutes. They just turned a cold shoulder to me. As it turned out I ended up becoming super famous around the world because of the controversy, but saying goodbye to a seven figure Nike contract was not an easy thing to do. They dropped me so quickly. There they were with me at the awards ceremony when I got my medal. The next day when the controversy hit I never heard from them again, after a 10 year relationship. They ended all communication. It was hard not to take that personally because I was at the peak of my career, I won a gold medal and within 24 hours I was in a Japanese jail. And although I went through the Court of Arbitration and got my medal back, it was too late.

> the relationships I'd built up over a long period of time... disintegrated within minutes

faris yakob

EVP, Chief Technology Strategist at McCann Erickson New York

Faris is EVP, Chief Technology Strategist at McCann Erickson New York, striving to better integrate brands, people and technology. Previously he spent 5 years as the 'Digital Ninja' at communication strategy shop Naked Communications.

Faris' 'Talent Imitates, Genius Steals' blog was placed by Campaign in their top ten advertising blogs in the UK and is currently the number 2 advertising planning blog in the world. He was also named a Campaign 'Face to Watch' in January 2008.

And now a word from our patrons….

When the age of mass media dawned, before advertising entered its fabled golden age in the late 50s and 60s, sponsorship was advertising. Radio created a mass audience, homogenizing cultural output, creating superstars, and advertisers wanted in. Direct commercial interruption – advertising – was felt to be too intrusive, so brands instead owned and controlled the content itself, indicated by the names: Champion Spark Plug Hour, The Voice of Firestone. Advertising agencies created them, as they later did for television.

Content was created to aggregate certain kinds of audiences to sell certain kinds of products. The relationship changed – networks wanted control of the content, and advertisers found it increasingly expensive to underwrite shows themselves. Thus, spot advertising, a model taken from magazines, was born.

Sponsorship as we think of it today has a much older heritage. Ancient Athenians would put up the funding for cultural and sporting events to make them accessible to the common man. In return they would get their name in stone. Royalty and aristocracy would provide patronage, for a combination of altruistic and image reasons, that allowed art to be created and events for the masses to happen. The nature of this commercial relationship was culturally defined – it was never a simple commercial transaction. It was, for want of a better word, subtler than simply sticking your name on something. A patron's sophistication and grace were reflected in how the patronage would manifest.

Today, brands provide patronage, but often forget it's not just their money that should be evident. When we think of sponsorships, we tend to think of events or properties. Inherent in the word is the idea that the event being sponsored exists exogenous to the brand – otherwise it is a brand event, not a sponsored one. The patronage should be fitting. Let's call this strategic coherence. The Vans Warped Tour makes sense – skate brand for skater music. However it can also be used to create relevance: Sprite sponsoring the X-Games establishes, rather than reinforces, Sprite's positioning. But beyond that, a patronage property should be treated with respect, and the brand's involvement should demonstrate its taste, its point of view. It should reflect the role of the brand in the world and its customers' lives – adding to the experience if appropriate, remaining discrete if not. When Pabst Blue Ribbon sponsored Bike messenger parties and events it did not slap banners over everything, it was simply supporting a culture that had championed its beer.

In almost every arena of culture, brand involvement is now present and necessary. Decrying the commercialization of culture is pointless – someone has to pay for it, especially if it is to reach larger audiences. Instead, as brand collaborators, we should all endeavor to ensure brand patronage demonstrates intelligence as well as assets.

> the brand's involvement should demonstrate its point of view… reflect the role of the brand in the world and its customers' lives

charlie hiscocks

Group Director of Brand Communications at SABMiller plc

Charlie Hiscocks is Group Director of Brand Communications at SABMiller plc, currently the second largest brewer in the world with more than 70 breweries in 45+ markets and c US$20 billion of annual sales.

Before joining SABMiller Charlie had 19 years' experience in agencies, including JWT, BBH and Ogilvy. His last agency job was as a co-founder of Tempus Partners.

Charlie is married with three children.

I don't like the word sponsorship, I prefer strategic alliance. Sponsorship rings of handing over cash and logos being splattered on things, of corporate largesse and patronage and just buying exposure. The best of sponsorship is a lot more sophisticated than that, and more to do with mutual benefit.

Great strategic alliances like these require partnership between brand and the rights owner. But some of the big sports organisations are incredibly arrogant, and often the start point of the conversation is 'we have the availability to take on a shirt sponsor and the price is this much money'. That isn't a strategic alliance.

Too many rights sellers are only interested in the rights fee. The good ones can see beyond the cheque, but in the beer business we get a lot of properties who tell us, we're willing to entertain offers and you have three weeks to put together your bid. That's not the right start point: if you're prepared to pay us we might be prepared to carry your logo, and by the way you can sell beer in our ground.

The punters understand the rules of the game. They can smell ego and lack of integrity from a million paces and likewise they can sense authenticity and transparency. They don't buy in to the idea that just because a sponsor is paying they should turn around and love them for it.

The nature of influence and persuasion is changing with the dramatic changes in technology. In terms of messaging and content the role of brands is also changing. In the future the great brands will be built on a simple compelling truth, but will also share a common interest with their public, forming exclusive alliances, which may be large or small in scope, in which they can work together with partners to achieve their individual and collective objectives.

The O2 is a tremendous example of an alliance with the venue owner / operator, which is being used as both a strategic and commercial tool. It clearly has a strong branding element but it is the added customer service dimension that has been laid across the top that I think is most impressive: priority booking for their customers, internal staff incentives, entertaining clients. It is very relevant for a phone operator to be able to take advantage of mobile ticketing. And it works because, similar to the work that Red Bull does, the partnership is the brand brought to life. I'm not an O2 customer, our company scheme is with another provider. But I'd like to be.

punters... can smell ego and lack of integrity from a million paces

defining sponsorship

So where to start?

The only definition that's readily available is from the European Sponsorship Association and this paints a compelling picture: rights, exchanged for money, delivering value for brands.

'Any commercial agreement by which a sponsor, for the mutual benefit of the sponsor and sponsored party, contractually provides financing or other support in order to establish an association between the sponsor's image, brands or products and a sponsorship property in return for rights to promote this association and/or for the granting of certain agreed direct or indirect benefits.'

this definition of sponsorship is the model as defined by the rights-sellers

Sounds legal. Mutual benefit, financing or other support, rights, association, direct or indirect benefits.

But the drafting sucks.

The same definition applies equally well to licensing. Or product placement. Or, for that matter, a straight media buy. The definition itself reveals much of our way of thinking about sponsorship, especially the lynchpin of 'rights'. Rights, exchanged for money, deliver value for sponsors. Precisely the paradigm for selling sponsorship.

TV rights, naming rights, image rights, usage rights, pouring rights, all have to be defined and understood. The ability to leverage partner assets is an essential and defining component of sponsorship. But rights have become the tail wagging the dog. Sponsorship's claim to fame is the scale of rights payments. The cost of branding Man U's shirt, the Ferrari F1 team, Dubai's new airport or David Beckham's new haircut is what drives coverage. The sponsorship economy.

This definition of sponsorship is the model as defined by the rights-sellers, who have a vested interest in the corporate world continuing to believe that sponsorship resides exclusively in the unsurpassable rights of the top and middle tier properties. The World Cup, Champion's League, the Olympics and F1 downwards.

And it's incredibly limited – and limiting. Not only does it fail to define sponsorship definitively, it misses the essence of sponsorship, the essence which, if managed well, makes sponsorship so unique and powerful.

So let's shoot for something better. A priori, as it were.

sponsor: rights-holder?

The first given in any sponsorship is a relationship, a relationship between two parties. Although the definition talks of sponsor and sponsored party, as an industry we tend to call them sponsor and rights-holder.

If, for the time being, we assume the word sponsor is a placeholder for a brand, what exactly is a rights-holder? Classically, we're talking about a sporting organisation such as FIFA or a cultural institution such as the Berlin Philharmonic. But a rights-holder, intrinsically, is anyone in possession of any sort of IP or 'rights', which includes NGOs, community-based initiatives, governments, media owners, you, me and pretty well anything, including other brands.

When Simon Thompson talks of a partnership between Motorola and D&G, both very strong brands, he's clearly talking of a relationship which is very different from the average sponsorship. But back in the late 90s, when Vans were managing their Triple Crown series – surf, BMX, moto X, skate etc – they were the rights-holder in an extensive web of brand relationships. Ferrari's partnership with Shell goes back 50 years. The only question relevant to fans is not: which one is the rights-holder, but: how good is my experience of these partnerships?

a rights-holder, intrinsically, is anyone in possession of any sort of IP or 'rights', which includes NGOs, community-based initiatives, governments, media owners, you, me and pretty well anything, including other brands.

The term rights-holder loses even more shape when we consider that most brands possess an equivalent, or stronger set of rights than most rights-holders. As Peter Franklin points out, Coke is serving over a billion portions of its products every day and its rights extend into relationships, media and commercially valuable IP in every country on the planet.

And conversely, rights-holders are brands as well, although, when it comes to consumer franchise, most sporting organisations don't even register on the same scale as the brand brands.

So brands are automatically rights-holders – and rights-holders are of necessity brands. Where does that leave us?

In principle, partners.

the relationship

But if we accept that rights-holders are brands and brands are rights-holders, need that fundamentally affect the sponsor – rights-holder dynamic that exists in most sponsorships? The implicit configuration of one partner (the brand) needing to derive benefits; and the other partner (the rights-holder) providing the solution.

Absolutely. The very term rights-holder implies a buyer-seller relationship, but the truth is, the relationship does not need to involve money, providing it's reciprocally beneficial. Rights-holders intrinsically need precisely the same things a brand does: brand equity, customer franchise, revenue. Although the industry has been configured for a sponsor to 'provide financing' to a sponsored party, this is neither a contingent, nor a defining characteristic.

I remember pitching to McDonalds back in the late 80s, on behalf of a not for profit. Even then, I was told, quite bluntly, that McDonalds owned more media than I could ever offer and that I would be lucky not to have to pay them to sponsor me. At the time it seemed the height of arrogance, but of course it was true. Rights fees are the big attraction of sponsorship, but for any rights-holder genuinely interested in developing a property, it is not necessarily the most important contribution: brand media, association, promotion and IP can be of significantly greater value.

Although a power differential will often exist, at a brand-to-brand or brand-to-cause level, partnership is more genuinely the paradigm, but the sponsor – rights-holder relationship has long been fraught. Peter Wells even argues that 'rights-holders get in the way'…

the industry has been configured for a sponsor to 'provide financing'

Despite positive intentions - Phillipe Le Floc'h talks of Heineken's UCL trophy tour as an example of partnership at work and many brand contributors describe sponsorship clearly in terms of partnering - for most rights-holders, the idea of partnership doesn't really extend beyond money plus.

The idea of a cashless association which builds a rights-holder proposition is ... a rarity. When Barcelona FC put Unicef on its shirt, and Honda put the earth on its car, both were significant in the sense of rights-holders actively attempting to build their brands. Regardless of execution, both acts represent progressive thinking.

Conversely, many brands fail to commit, in earnest, to sponsorship. Rights fees are swallowed like a bitter pill, sweetened by the assumption that the rights will work their magic.

Either way, everyone loses, because the relationship only has meaning if viewed through the eyes of the consumer.

genuine value-add

The relationship has to deliver genuine value-add for consumers. Both parties carry a responsibility to manage consumer touchpoints with a sponsorship and both parties are judged on the experience. Both parties need to be able to lay legitimate claim to enhancing the consumer experience. In order to deliver against brand potential, any sponsor, reverting briefly to that terminology, has to do something worthwhile.

Funding some events or institutions can be worthwhile in its own right. The sponsors of the Globe in London, for example, deserve thanks and loyalty in the Faris Yakob / Alain de Botton sense of having provided beneficent patronage. However, despite every fan survey conducted by the validation industry on behalf of rights-holders, which consistently report that consumers prefer brand marketing spend to be invested into sponsorship than other marketing activity - the gratitude model of sponsorship is largely a thing of the past. Tony Ponturo shares that Budweiser's own research shows clear consumer resistance to badging.

For major financial entities such as Man U or FIFA, sponsor investment is at best an irrelevance for consumers. Andy Walsh argues for a clear fan benefit from sponsor funding and his position is well put. That's not to say he's necessarily right in how sponsor revenue should be deployed, but he represents a legitimate consumer perspective about how sponsorship revenue should be used. And increasing rights-holder profitability is not one of those uses.

> the brand is modelling its vision of consumers - if there is no real value to the sponsor's presence, the brand is modelling itself as superfluous, disengaged, impersonal, aloof, take your pick

So the relationship has to add genuine value in consumers' perceptions for it to fulfil its potential - the old truism with a new vigour. After all, the brand is modelling its vision of consumers. If there is no real value to the sponsor's presence, the brand is modelling itself as superfluous, disengaged, impersonal, aloof, take your pick.

Optimally, the sponsor will have a genuine role to play and products or services will be an integrated element of the experience. As Peter Franklin says for Coca-Cola: 'there has to be a particular role for us to play.. something… unique for us ….to triangulate between our brand and the passion consumers have for the property'. Failing that, the sponsor can still demonstrate its values in the way it interacts with consumers. Sorry, people.

It's easy for activation to remain token, tinkering around the edges rather than fundamentally addressing consumer experience. For brands which ignore this fundamental truth, sponsorship is likely to be damaging.

Because the very heart of sponsorship is about the brand.

brand play

At the heart of sponsorship has to be a brand play.

The slow tide of contemporary brand awareness which began in the 80s continues to rise, and is still infiltrating even B2B sectors which stubbornly resisted the brand concept; and with that the understanding that every single thing you do as a brand is an expression of your values.

Branding agencies help businesses to develop a clear brand proposition, and ensure coherent branding, internally and externally, through language, imagery, product, customer relations, employee relations, everything, because, from a holistic brand perspective, everything counts.

The same applies to sponsorship. Sponsorship offers brands the opportunity to model their values and promise in a fresh context. But it's not just the property that carries the brand. It's the tone of voice, the production values, the promotional mechanics, the activation concepts, the participation mechanisms, the relationship gradient with consumers, everything.

Strategic sponsorship takes businesses into areas of life far removed from their norm. When Telefonica sponsors the Davis Cup, it's because it wants to create an alternative strand of dialogue with consumers. The reason it exposes itself in an alien environment is because this change of context offers the potential for greater prominence for its values, allowing consumers to appraise the brand afresh. Stripped from a commercial context, every action in a sponsorship context amplifies the brand dimension. In Martin Lindstrom's words: sponsorship works when we are not aware of the signals being sent.

It is part of the fallacy of the power of association that the values of the rights-holder rub off on the brand. The sponsorship industry has always talked of 'brand value transfer' flowing towards the brand, but this is only a part of the story. Vodafone's association with Lewis Hamilton only works because Vodafone walks and talks like a world leader. There is undoubtedly value transfer from Lewis Hamilton, but only if Vodafone acts like Vodafone. If 3 were the sponsor, Lewis Hamilton's image would be the poorer. The sponsor is primarily responsible for the brand take-out by consumers.

it is part of the fallacy of the power of association that the values of the rights-holder rub off on the brand

As Kevin Roberts puts it: what does women's tennis bring to Sony Ericsson in terms of involvement and enrichment or happiness or purpose to the base proposition?

It continues to surprise us that brands can labour over carefully and expensively crafted brand promises and customer propositions, which they apply coherently through traditional media. And yet, when they come to sponsorship, they sign off a rough value fit and a logo.

value fit

Values offer an essential filter for platform and property selection, of course: you don't sponsor an individual if you're about teamwork, obviously.

But in our experience, the industry still applies a very loose model of alignment between brand and rights-holder values, with fairly superficial profiling exercises calling out alignment, typically against generic values such as dynamic, passionate, professional, flexible etc.

These exercises typically also focus single mindedly on the 'positive' associations, ignoring the value dimensions of an association which aren't quite so positive. Vodafone understands that, in order to communicate leadership, coming second is not an option.

Leaving to one side the basic criticism that the generic adjectives of the sort often used in these exercises are insufficient to really define a brand; and the disbelief that so many brands still hope to differentiate themselves by using such generic values - simple value alignment is not the end-point.

Any brand entering into sponsorship should only do so if it is absolutely clear that the association is capable of carrying either the brand proposition itself, or a close derivative.

any brand entering into sponsorship should only do so if it is absolutely clear that the association is capable of carrying either the brand proposition itself, or a close derivative

For most brands whose products are not genuinely integrated into the delivery of Formula 1 – most of them – there is limited communications potential. If you win, it says: we're a leader. If you don't, it says: we've got a lot of money. Enough to burn.

'Priceless' is an example of where this is heading. The sense of priceless in MasterCard's above the line is different from that in Mastercard's sponsorships, but at least the sponsorships verbally support the brand proposition, which can be used to create parameters for activation. For the consumer, it is possible to see priceless running through all brand comms.

'Red Bull gives you wings' is even better: the tagline clearly shapes the DNA of all sponsorship, from local to global.

But that same easy-fit mentality that's applied to values also gets applied to audience.

passion?

In the clichéd sales parlance of sponsorship, we're talking … passion. Passionate fans… of tennis, of footie, of F1. Salivating at the opportunity to buy sponsor products. Passion became the buzzword of the 90s and still hasn't disappeared. Passion is implicitly what all fans feel about their favourite sport / team / personality. And 'passion drivers' is how Octagon frames its insight into the emotional world of the fan.

But the sales rhetoric is often the most passionate part. Again, it's not difficult to understand why the word is so popularly linked to sponsorship - it's another part of the sales paradigm. The promise that, through your sponsorship, you are going to claim the undivided loyalty of fans has been implicit from the early days. And it's always been nonsense.

Fans of course can be passionate but, by and large, they're the ones you avoid. The impact of Michael Jordan on Ade Adepitan is impressive, but unusual. People aren't passionate about many things. You might be truly passionate about your football club but, boy, are you an exception. And if you're not in a majority as a footie fan, you're going to feel even lonelier if you're passionate about tennis. Let alone women's tennis.

The truth is, passion percentages don't add up.

There aren't enough subject-specific passionate people in the world to uphold the sponsorship model. Sailing in the UK, for example, claims a lifetime participation audience of 11% - that is, people who at one time in their lives have tried sailing. The percentage of Britons regularly sailing stands at 0.2%.
The percentage of people who care enough about sailing to be prepared to pay for sailing news stands at less than 0.01%.

So, unless you're selling yachts, 1% of this market is worth two thirds of diddly squat.

There aren't enough subject-specific passionate people in the world to uphold the sponsorship model. Sailing in the UK, for example, claims a lifetime participation audience of 11% - that is, people who at one time in their lives have tried sailing. The percentage of Britons regularly sailing stands at 0.1%. The percentage of people who will follow sailing in the news – and really care about it – stands at less than Y%, So, unless you're selling yachts, 1% of this market is worth two thirds of diddly squat.

sponsorship is not a shortcut to passion - sponsorship is a shortcut to relevance

Octagon's passion drivers' contribution is to acknowledge that consumers, people, have different kinds of relationships with their interests. But the passion driver framework is misleading. It suggests a line of passion running through all these diverse audiences, which really isn't there. As passion. Sponsorship is not a shortcut to passion. Sponsorship is a shortcut to relevance.

no, relevance

The challenge brands face, as Peter Wells identifies, is to ensure their relevance to consumers. Some brands, such as Apple, manage this through their product offering. Some brands, such as Pot Noodle, manage this through attitude. Many businesses are visibly attempting to maintain their relevance at the moment by addressing their green credentials.

Every four years, the World Cup is incredibly relevant. And the great thing about the World Cup is that it's growing more relevant. As society becomes more secular, the World Cup is occupying the space that religious festivals used to fill. Regardless of how passionately you feel about football, you can't fail to notice the holiday mood that covers the entire globe.

As individualism, as an ideal, reaches its apogee, we're fascinated as a society by the insights we're fed into the lives of celebrities; and the individual – as Simon Lowden and Nic Couchman argue – can offer broader relevance than most organisations.

sponsorship offers a route to relevance by permitting an alternative entry point into the consumer's world, where the brand has another opportunity to showcase itself and its values

Sponsorship offers a route to relevance by permitting an alternative entry point into the consumer's world, where the brand has another opportunity to showcase itself and its values: 'a contemporary feel', in the words of David Aaker. An entry point apart from product. Because even when brands are brave enough to conduct brand-led ATL, product is never too far away. And, as Martin Lindstrom points out, consumer perceptions are filtered and tainted by the proximity of the sell.

It's the eternal struggle of brands to remain relevant. But many sports actually have limited relevance. Content based on subject matter which has greater social and emotional relevance to consumers often offers brands more opportunities to interact with consumers on common ground.

Which is why the vision of contributors such as John Luff, David Butler, Giles Gibbons and Patrick Nally, surely one of the elders of the industry, will surely come to pass. This vision of brands committing to projects of social and community relevance aligns with the thoughts of Marc Gobé, Charlie Hiscocks and Sally Hancock, around the close identification of brands and audience interests. And when Kevin Roberts quotes David Ogilvy, and talks of fans being treated like morons, instead of people, he's making precisely the same point.

evaluation, validation

The Coke paradigm of sponsorship, according to Steve Cumming, is relationships and assets: sponsorship facilitates relationships and provides assets, which offer brands additional benefit: TV exposure, pouring rights, customer data, CRM content, relationship-building opportunities and much, much more.

David Wheldon gives a very clear example of why the TV exposure which accompanies a few sponsorships can be extremely valuable: for any brand entering into new markets, sponsorship can generate exceptional levels of awareness.

But the essence of sponsorship is not based on TV exposure, or assets. It's based on relevance, and Kevin Roberts' evaluation challenge to the industry, although it's not new, remains very pertinent. It's not about eyeballs.

Most sponsorship evaluations are exercises in validation. Most of the evaluation reports we've seen applied to our clients' sponsorships don't even distinguish between business objectives and campaign objectives. How well did we manage the campaign versus what contribution did the campaign actually make to the business? Obviously, it's the client's choice if they want to use such data to validate their marketing investment. But the price for keeping evaluation such a comfortable exercise can only be a loss of integrity and credibility, a failure to learn and a waste of investment.

Media value is just the worst offender in the battery of validation techniques. Worst because, for most brands, logo exposure per se brings marginal benefit; and because the emphasis EAV places on logo exposure obscures the value of emotional connection.

We have worked with the econometrics teams of enough businesses now to be able to demonstrate a clear link between revenue – be that acquisition, retention, uplift – and sponsorship to know that clear, transparent evaluation is possible. There are only two obstacles: lack of data, and laziness. Tirelessly curious, it's difficult for us to conceive of a business too lazy to explore the impact of its marketing.

Vodafone track preference and ROI. Carlsberg measure direct sales. The point is, measurement is possible. And the correlation is generally positive. Sometimes surprisingly so.

most sponsorship evaluations are exercises in validation

sponsorship content

How then do we describe the actual stuff of sponsorship? Much sports sponsorship is event-led, but a refresher of Naomi Klein's 'No Logo' reminds us that absolutely anything can be sponsored, so 'form' is not a starting point.

We could talk in terms of content. Content is popular at the moment: branded content, user generated content, exclusive content, the variations are endless. But we're not talking downloadable digital imagery or sound, not even AFP. Instead, we're talking within the context created by Peter Wells and Mark Earls: anything which stimulates social content, an interesting conversation.

sponsorship IP can range from a tangible commercial property such as the Olympic Games; a brand promise brought alive through sponsored assets; to a simple proposition; and everything in between

It's an analogy which many content-hungry brands should bear in mind. You could be mistaken for thinking that some brands have changed their business model into content-ownership. Unless they have, the value of content is no more and no less than to enable conversations with customers.

The term IP is perhaps less confusing. Sponsorship IP can range from a tangible commercial property such as the Olympic Games, to a simple proposition; such as Nike's Joga Bonito; and everything in between.

When Steve Cumming talks of IP in the context of Diageo, he cites Johnny Walker's keep walking and anti-drink-driving activities, both differentiating IP positions. When Paul Meulendijk talks of an overarching theme, in the context of Master-Card, Priceless is intended to be the underlying IP which defines sponsorship content and activation.

So where does that IP stop and start? John Luff, Giles Gibbons, David Butler and Lesa Ukman all talk of sponsorship from a different perspective: sponsorship which has broader community relevance, sponsorship which does good. Is this sponsorship or corporate responsibility? From a business perspective, CR and sponsorship often sit in offices at opposite ends of the building.

The Body Shop's campaign against domestic violence, back in the mid '90s, is an interesting case study: a campaign created by The Body Shop, it co-opted NGOs around the world to raise a subject skirted at the time even by government, and demonstrated very deep consumer insight – as well as immense brand confidence. Remember 'No advertising'?

This would typically be labelled corporate responsibility, but in every respect it behaves like sponsorship – based on partnership, relevance, shared assets, consumer engagement and more.

The point is: sponsorship is truly platform-neutral.

two cheers

Redmandarin has always prided itself on being, not advocates for sponsorship, but advocates for good sponsorship. Good sponsorship, we believe, has the potential to build brands and drive marketing programmes.

And we're not alone. A goodly number of contributors – from the brand side – are passionate about sponsorship. Curiously enough, they're all ex-advertising, and their marketing evolution all follows a similar pattern: from cynic to zealot.

Trying to separate out the perception of brands such as Vodafone, Coca-Cola, Pepsi and Carlsberg from their sponsorship is impossible, it's played such a fundamental role in communicating the brands. Take a look at Interbrand's top 100 global brands and try again. And some sponsorship are genuinely business-transformational: association with the IOC helped elevate Visa and Samsung into global superbrands.

Denial of sponsorship's potential is to deny a powerful marketing tool, and in some ways, an entire approach to marketing.

But this is only two cheers for sponsorship.

Along with Keld Strudahl, Charlie Hiscocks and Steve Cumming, we feel the word sponsorship itself creates bad associations. Ironic. Ironic that we've collectively mismanaged the sponsorship brand. The industry is repeatedly subject to the charge of being profligate, unaccountable and whimsical.

Blunt denial is not the answer: we have to ask ourselves why these associations exist.

If we, the sponsorship industry, are going to achieve the recognition for sponsorship it deserves, we need to lobby for higher standards of corporate governance. Who ultimately can authorise sponsorship? And what is the process required to ensure sponsorship is a strategic investment?

We need to acknowledge that some sponsorship – as much as advertising, sales promotion, DM – can be bad, wasteful, and profligate. Keld Strudahl's stance of constant self-criticism is a path to self-awareness, something which sponsorship can run dangerously short of.

> **a goodly number of contributors are passionate about sponsorship - curiously enough, they're all ex-advertising and their marketing evolution follows a similar pattern: from cynic to zealot**

new model?

Patrick Nally leads the way again, with his clarity: the traditional, packaged rights model of sponsorship is dying.

The new model already exists of course. And has done for many years.

Red Bull proved beyond doubt that a clear positioning, a clear identification with audience and attitude can grow a brand sufficiently to build a strong franchise. Quiksilver, Billabong, Ripcurl and O'Neill did it in the 60s. Sony Playstation did the same in the mid 90s. The Body Shop did it for 20 years. Nike has long been exploring IP.

the new model is earn the association, recognising that all that sponsorship can provide – potentially – is a reason to believe

• a tight proposition for all events

• partnering the sports (often in the form of the leading exponents, rather than the governing bodies), to create events which have always been absolutely on the pulse of the sport

• amazing audience insight, understanding the aspirations of the stars of these new sports and helping to translate them into reality, creating a vastly enhanced experience for fans

• media exposure which assumed fragmentation from the outset and built itself, gradually, on truly unique visual content

• multiple small properties, run to a culturally well-defined DNA, with brand-owned events generally starting small scale, low risk, trialling new styles and disciplines

The old model is to buy an association and activate, assuming the association buys you the right to activate. The new model is earn the association, recognising that all that sponsorship can provide – potentially – is a reason to believe. It is always the responsibility of the sponsor to deliver against that reason to believe. The new model of sponsorship works harder.

As Marc Gobé hammers home – it's all about credibility, nothing else. And for all of Red Bull's blatant self-promotion, its insight into the sports and their audiences always safeguarded more than enough credibility for the brand.

But the real 'new model' is far bigger.

Sponsorship is far from being just a channel, and it's more than a discipline. It's a mindset, an approach to marketing in its own right.

Intrinsically integrated, multi-channel, content-led, engaging 3-dimensionally with consumers to build brand engagement.

No wonder advertising's always been nervous.

towards re-definition

The old definition is increasingly ill-fitting, a memory, not a vision for the industry. It's time for a new one.

Or, at least, the discussion.

For Redmandarin, sponsorship is a model for integrated marketing which:

• deploys the organisational assets of two or more partners
• offers brands the opportunity to model their promise and values in areas of social and/or emotional relevance
• has as its primary focus the deepening of relationships with consumers

Perfect? No. But for us, it feels much closer to the mark. The emphasis feels right.

sponsorship is a model for integrated marketing

It applies equally to the great history of sponsorship deals: Coca-Cola and the IOC, Shell and Ferrari, Horst Dassler and the creation of FIFA rights; as it does to the new era of brand-led sponsorships: Red Bull's Flugtag / air race, Nike's Joga Bonita.

Is this so very far from the ESA definition quoted at the beginning? Is this all just nitpicking? Yes and no. The basic ingredients of sponsorship can't change: what's important is the emphasis and priority given to each. This is bolognese with more meat and less tomatoes. More Caffe Nero, and less Starbucks. The nature, the intent and the focus of the relationship are more important than the number of partners, and what the transactional component of their relationship might (or might not) be.

This definition is based on our attempt to discern what lies at the absolute heart of sponsorship. Of good sponsorship, in other words. There are plenty of deals which fit the old definition better than this one.

We just don't think they live up to the promise of strategic.

shaun.whatling@redmandarin.com

Thanks to everyone over the years who's
made Redmandarin what it is.
We've still got your photos!
Huge thanks to our fabulous designer,
AlexisBainger@gmail.com and to Alice,
for helping pull this all together.